PRAISE FOR RAISING REAL MEN

"In a time when our culture seems intent on emasculating our boys, it is a real pleasure to find Christians who are pushing back, responding with biblical answers. *Raising Real Men* combines a number of important characteristics in giving advice to parents of young boys — **it is earthy, realistic, humorous and scriptural.** Hal and Melanie Young write from a homeschooling setting, but much of what they have to say is also pertinent to Christian parents of boys in private Christian schools. I hope this book gets a wide reading in both realms."

Douglas Wilson
Minister of Christ Church, Moscow, Idaho
Author, *Future Men*

"As the grandfather of six boys ranging in age from two to fifteen, I am acutely aware of the need that this book fills, and quite admirably. **This is just what the doctor ordered for parents who want to raise capable Christian men of character.**"

John Rosemond
Author, *Parenting by The Book*

"*Raising Real Men* is for real men who aspire to pass on a legacy of strength, courage and fidelity to Christ our King. **It encouraged me as a father. I pray it will encourage you.**"

Dr. R.C. Sproul, Jr.
Teacher, Author, *When You Rise Up*
Husband of One and Father of Seven Blessings

"Raising boys can be a tremendous challenge for parents, especially when you have more than a few. Hal and Melanie in *Raising Real Men* have approached this subject from a Biblical perspective and ... bring a unique practical aspect to raising boys where the rubber meets the road. **This is a book that every family should have no matter the number of boys and even those families without boys** as the book gives tremendous insight into understanding how boys think and why they act as they do. **This book meets a crying need in an area where there is very little specific direction.** Thank you Hal and Melanie for this outstanding work of the Lord."

J. Michael Smith, Esq.
President, Home School Legal Defense Association

"Hal and Melanie Young have written a delightful book for the parents of boys. With biblical insight and lessons learned from raising six sons of their own, they have provided **a treasure trove of practical wisdom for dads and moms who are blessed with the challenge of helping boys become men.** Entertainment, education, risk, leadership, spirituality, violence, vocation and finances are some of the topics that addressed. In a day of sexual confusion and a widespread feminization of our culture, sage counsel on masculinity and ways to train young men in it is both needed and welcome."

Tom Ascol
Executive Director, Founders Ministries

"**Principled, practical, and persuasive**, this is a book I would recommend to anyone who is interested in learning more about what boys are all about."

Sen. Kevin Lundberg
Colorado State Senate

"Wow. *Raising Real Men* is one of those books that you'll read through quickly, then go back to use as a reference. It's full of anecdotes, resources, suggestions — and one-liners; with no pop psychology! **Pastors should read this book and recommend it to families — whether they have sons or daughters.**"

Rev. Dr. J. Curtis and Sandra Lovelace
Lifework Forum

"Pam and I have ten children — seven boys and three girls. The oldest is thirty-two years old and the youngest is only a year old. That fact gives us a perspective that most people do not have ...

When I first picked up Raising Real Men and read, "Young boys can be downright destructive." I knew that this was going to be a book that was not only entertaining and challenging but also truthful. For you see, Richardson boys can be downright destructive too!

Hal and Melanie have done what few people are willing to do. **They have opened their hearts and lives and allowed us to see what is really on the inside. They have dropped all their barricades and defenses for the sole purpose of helping you and me to raise our children to be Real Men.** They teach that we must see our children's potential — not just their potential to work — their potential to become mighty in spirit — men who will come along beside us and after us, having a real and godly impact on this world and reaching many for Jesus Christ.

It is my hope and prayer that reading Raising Real Men will give you a vision for raising sons who are protectors, persistent, honorable and obedient."

Mike Richardson
Missionary in Mexico, Publisher of *El Hogar Educador*

"Hal and Melane Young have six sons and are disciples of Jesus. They know how to raise real men. This book is a treasure trove of practical tips to help you to raise your sons right. **It will answer your questions, help you avoid mistakes, bring them up in the Lord, and understand them. I highly recommend it.**"

"I highly recommend this book to all parents of boys. It's filled with informative tips concerning the challenges and rewards of parenting sons. **God has gifted Hal and Melanie with great insights about raising young men.**"

"Hal and Melanie have put together a **wonderful, warm-hearted, and practical** little book on raising sons into men of God—**a must-read for any parent blessed with boys.**"

"**Hal and Melanie Young have their finger on the pulse of what it takes to grow confident, strong, godly young men who will be ready to take on the world at a young age.** Mothers of boys who read *Raising Real Men* will be challenged and affirmed...learning to co-mentor our sons as they move toward their callings and divine destinies, being launched, one by one, like flaming arrows into eternity."

Raising Real Men

Be strong and courageous !
Josh 1.9

Hal Young

Raising Real Men

Surviving, Teaching and Appreciating Boys

Hal and Melanie Young

GREAT WATERS PRESS

SMITHFIELD LEXINGTON LIBERTY HILL

WWW.GREATWATERSPRESS.COM

Raising Real Men

Publisher's Cataloging-in-Publication Data

Young, Hal, 1964.
 Raising real men: surviving, teaching and appreciating boys./ Hal and Melanie Young
  p. cm.
 ISBN-10: 0-9841443-0-7 (trade paperback)
 ISBN-13: 978-0-9841443-0-3 (trade paperback)
  1. Parenting - Religious aspects - Christianity. 2. Boys - Religious life. 3. Masculinity - Religious aspects - Christianity. I. Young, Melanie. II. Title.
 BV4529.Y68
 248.8'45 — dc21
 Library of Congress Control Number: 2009908989

DEDICATION

In all fairness, who else could we dedicate this book to but

John Calvin Young
Caleb McLeod Young
Matthew Henry Young
Samuel Adams Young
Seth Harral Young
and
David Brainerd Young,

our six sons.

You have been God's gift and inheritance to us, and His means
to teach us so much about His love, His grace, His providential
care, and His patience toward all of His children, especially us.
May He richly bless each of you
and the tribes you one day found.

But we would be remiss to omit

Susannah Ruth Young
and
Katherine Luther Young,

our daughters,
who are teaching us a new set of lessons
about God's mysterious ways.

May you, too, be blessed with joy and abundance
of God's mercy and love.

CONTENTS

Introduction

The Challenge of Boys

Maybe we should have expected it. If we had looked around our extended family and really noticed that Hal's family only had two girls out of ten cousins, and on Melanie's side, two girls out of six, we might have guessed we'd be likely to have boys. In fact, if we had known more of our family history, we'd have been convinced of it—since the Civil War, both sides of our family have tended that way, boys outnumbering girls two to one. But since both our childhood families consisted of the Dick-and-Jane stereotype of Mom and Dad and one boy and one girl, it never occurred to us to think about it.

And now we have six.

"*Six boys!*" the people at the checkout line say in mock horror. Yes, we say, and smile warmly. "Well, better *you* than *me*," they conclude, shaking their heads. To be fair, not everyone reacts this way. Some cultures seem to place a special value on sons. Our Kenyan-born obstetrician used to beam at our three boys then and say, "Ah, you will have *another son.*" His Jamaican wife, his head nurse, would demur, "Oh, no, they'll have a *sweet little girl.*" "No!" he'd say. "They will have *sons.*" We hear young Hispanic men in line behind us at the grocery store, counting quietly under their breath—" ... *cuatro—cinco—*seis niños!" and when Melanie turns around and confirms, "*Sí, seis niños!*" —nearly the total of her Spanish vocabulary—there are smiles all around.

15

Too often, though, we hear the negative wisecracks from our fellow Americans, and far too often, from our fellow Christians. We have a few snappy comebacks of our own if someone is remarkably crude, but usually we try to answer with grace and cheerfulness. We defend our decision to have a large family and we especially express our happiness to be the parents of many sons. The nerve of people, we say to ourselves, who think there's open season to make public remarks about other people's private affairs. And in front of the children — *their own* children — to announce how burdensome kids are.

Behold, children are a heritage from the LORD, *the fruit of the womb is a reward,* says the Psalmist, or as one of the psalters rendered it, *Lo, children are the Lord's good gift / Rich payment are men's sons; / The sons of youth as arrows are / In hands of mighty ones.*[1] The world pities us, but God says He has blessed us. Why, in the Old Testament God gave Heman *fourteen* sons *to exalt* him.[2] We stand up to the world's attitudes and smart remarks with confidence.

But back at home, privately, we admit to ourselves it's not always rosy. The jokes sometimes have an element of truth to them. Yes, teenaged boys can put away a startling amount of groceries. Young boys can be downright destructive. They tend to be noisy at any age. They seem utterly unconcerned with personal hygiene. The dog has a longer attention span for schoolwork.

Worse, they seem to come forth at birth with a chip on their shoulder. They are combative, aggressive, arrogant. They seem obsessed with power — whether powerful machines, powerful weapons, or personal power they can exert over people and things. They love to build things but have a perverse delight in tearing them down, and if fire and explosion come into the mix, surely boy-nirvana is close at hand. The older bullies the younger; the younger schemes to entrap the older; the middle son plays two ends against the middle for the joy of ratting out both of them. The youngest are like bantam roosters, strutting and posturing; they grow into wild bulls, crushing china, furniture, and family members without even noticing the havoc in their wake.

Or so it seems, some days.

If this is God's chosen gift to us, and He says that it is, then why does it seem so *hard*?

Is it them or is it me? How can I prepare these boys for a life serving God when we can barely make it through the day? Isn't there a better way?

The answer is *yes*.

Raising Real Men

Several years ago, Melanie was asked to share her thoughts about raising and homeschooling boys. It seemed to be a straightforward matter, describing things we had found effective with our growing family and passing along some biblical principles we had been shown along the way.

Much to our surprise, the response she received went beyond appreciative — it was enthusiastic, tinged with an unexpected note of desperation from many in the audience. As she has spoken since then, the same thing has occurred — mothers and even an occasional father, streaming to the front afterward to thank her for giving them a new perspective on their boys. There seems to be an unmet need in many families for understanding and learning to appreciate these energetic beings so different from their sisters — and from the mother who is trying to raise and teach them. While there is a special bond between mother and child, there is also a dynamic between this mature female and this immature male that wasn't covered in the books we read during premarital counseling.

This book does not outline a Five Stage Program for Building Godly Men. It does not feature a Master Checklist to Chart Your Way to Family Harmony. There are programs like that which some families find very effective, while others find them less than helpful.

What this book offers is a biblical perspective — note "a", not "the" — on understanding how boys think, and why that is, and what can and should be done about it. As we've raised our sons, we've found that many of the troubles and concerns we had were clarified when we looked to what God intended them to be. The situation looked different when we truly valued manly virtues and masculinity and when we understood that we had to rebuke sin but should not change our boys into something they were not. In a culture frought with gender confusion, classic boyhood has become increasingly problematic. How sad to be someone that provokes pity for your parents. Boyhood shouldn't be that way. We've learned to appreciate our boys, to enjoy their manhood, while spurring them on to holiness and godliness. We want you to feel that way, too. We hope we'll all raise real men that are pleasing to God.

We don't have degrees in Boy Psychology or Applied Biblical Theology of Hyperactive Youth, but Hal is a former boy himself, while Melanie has spent the last twenty years nurturing them one after another. She has homeschooled as many as six, from grades K-12, at the same time, and we have had the pleasure of graduating one already as we start to line up the runway for the second. We should also mention that besides having a former girl, Melanie, at home, the sovereign God saw fit to bless us with two daughters late in the process. This book is not about them, though; we're still in a steep learning curve when it comes to raising girls. We also don't apologize much for the longstanding email address, *youngandsons*, that finally begged explanation many years after we invented it. When everyone is grown and married, Lord willing, there will be twelve Youngs and four of other names in this generation, taking another step toward the prediction of Hal's father, who once said, "Youngs and crabgrass will take over the world." So the email stays.

We hope you'll stay, too, and gain perspective that will help you not only to survive, but delight in raising your boys. We think that as you understand how God has designed a boy, as you begin to look past the untied shoes and jeans he's been wearing for a week and see the man he's trying to become, that you'll gain new purpose, patience and joy in your sons. Let's go!

Notes

1 Psalm 127:3-4; the metrical setting of Psalm 127 is from *The Book of Psalms for Singing*, (c) 1973 Crown & Covenant Publications, 7408 Penn Ave., Pittsburgh, PA 15208-2531. Used by permission..

2 1 Chronicles 25:5. Note that the exalted Heman ended up with seventeen children, which is the basis for another interesting discussion.

PART ONE

VIRTUES IN THE ROUGH

The little lad watched longingly as his big brothers climbed the steep path beside the waterfall while he waited safe on the bridge below with his mother.

"Mom, can I go, too?"

"No, son, it's not safe!" she said.

"Then can I please, please, *please* climb up to just that tree there?"

Her heart quailed as she pictured him slipping and sliding onto the hard rocks.

"I'm afraid you'll fall. I don't want you to fall in the water. You don't have a change of clothes."

His face fell. He looked sad, even embarrassed. She realized that he was feeling left out of the men. All of his older brothers were climbing and taking risks and here he was, standing by Mom's side with the little girls.

She looked around for a climb that would allow her to compromise, to allow him to exert his growing manhood without taking too big a risk.

"How about if you climb up there?" she asked, pointing.

"Thanks, Mom!" he nearly shouted with joy, leaping to climb the hill. For him, it was a mountain, *his* mountain, and he was an adventurer! He was no longer the little boy clinging to Mama, he was a man with a lion's heart.

As the parents of boys, little decisions like this one impact our boys' views of themselves as men. It may not seem important to let your little ones take reasonable risks, but it is part of a principled attitude toward raising our boys to be real men, godly men, warriors for Christ. When David asked Melanie again and again if he could just climb to "there," she felt annoyed; after all, she just wanted to enjoy the waterfall, not worry about injured boys or damaged clothing or cutting short the family outing.

When she looked in his face, though, she realized what it meant to him and thought again about what she was doing. What message was he receiving from her decision to keep him at Mama's side, when what he wanted was to explore, to challenge, to conquer? What would he learn about his manhood by taking a calculated risk? Could it be the Lord would use this opportunity to build confidence in our sometimes fearful son? Could it be our son needed to think that Mom believed he was man enough to master something that seemed *dangerous*?

Probably so.

When we got back to the van, we found we'd left the keys in the ignition. Thankfully, the back doors were unlocked, though the rear of the van was packed to the roof with the furniture and belongings just moved out of our older son's dorm room. We thought for a moment of unpacking it all, there in the parking lot, for the amusement of the entire Blue Ridge Parkway.

"Maybe David could ooch across the top and rescue us!" Melanie suggested.

We made an opening, and David climbed up and slithered across the pile of chairs, books, refrigerator, boxes and junk. Safely in front, he unlocked the van for the rest of us, then returned to the back to peek through the opening like the leader of a successful mine rescue.

"Mom! Mom!" he shouted, to get her attention. "Mom, I did it! I rescued the family!" He couldn't have been prouder if he'd recovered both the trapped miners *and* the invaluable cache of giant diamonds.

"Thank you, David," Melanie said. "You're my hero! I would have been *so* embarrassed to sit here in the wilderness for hours, waiting on AAA because of my mistake." He glowed.

He was so happy to make a contribution, to be a rescuer, to be the little man of the family. How can we remember to look past the immediate situation and think about the long term effects of small decisions like whether to climb the waterfall?

A Marred Image

"Mommy? What do I look like?" the little boy said hopefully, on another day.

Well, that was a stumper. He was wrapped in a velvet king's robe, with an Australian bush hat on his head, sunglasses on his face, and a toy rifle in his hand.

Melanie answered, wisely, "You look great! Tell me about what you are pretending."

Just as she had a hard time figuring out what our son was representing, when we look at the foolishness and immaturity of our little boys we have a hard time recognizing the men they will become. God made man in His own image, yet that image has been marred by sin. Even the good things in our personality are damaged.

We really see this when we look at the things that give us a hard time with our sons. Take authority: Boys seem programmed to challenge it. Have you ever felt like you needed a holster for your paddle? Do you think about hiding switches all over the house to cut down on the walking? God has placed in our boys a desire to be in charge, because one day they *will* be in charge. Today's boys will be the fathers, and bosses, and elders, and statesmen of tomorrow. We've got to teach them how to submit to authority without destroying their leadership.

And the frenzied activity: All the time, it seems, mothers are calling concerned that their little boys are hyperactive. He just won't sit and color, his big sister was doing twelve workbook pages a day at his age and he spends three hours, even more, on just one. Doesn't he need to be on medication?

The proper answer is no, there is no treatment for being a little boy. With time, he will become a perfectly normal teenager.

So what are you going to do about it?

God made that little boy energetic so one day he could go out and conquer the world. At least, one day he'll have the gumption to support his family, minister in his church, be a pillar in his community. Right now, he just needs to learn some self-control.

But he's aggressive and loves to fight? One day he may be called to defend his country or protect his family. It's our job to make him a protector and not a bully.

But what about the dirt? Why do boys love dirt? And blood and guts and worms and insects? Because one day he might be waist-deep in a swamp, pulling your family out of a wrecked automobile. Or splattered with arterial blood while pioneering a new surgical procedure. Or eating roasted grub worms with the natives to earn their permission to share the Gospel. It might not be our cup o' tea, any of them, but would you rather have men able to overlook things like that for the higher business at hand — or would you prefer fastidious pseudo-men who are only good to wait for someone else to take care of it?

Boys - just like little girls - are a picture of the image of God, tragically marred by sin. Our focus must be on leading our sons into godly manhood, not just trying to manage them to make our lives convenient and more pleasant.

Resisting Feminization

Because undoubtedly it *would* be very convenient and pleasant if little boys would sit and color quietly like their sisters. Admit it. When the girls are quiet, all's sweetness and light. When the boys are quiet, *someone better check on them.*

"Convenient" is not part of the job description of parenting, nor of boyhood.

And while parents of girls will tell their own stories of the troubles girls bring, even the illusion of quiet, manageable *tractability* in girls has become a tool against boys. An ideal based on feministic ideas is used as a standard for men, too: look at magazines in the grocery store line. Heroism and confidence are passe; it's men who are sensitive, soft, self-doubting, *damaged* in some way, that get the media attention. Women are being encouraged to seduce men, while at the same time their maternal instincts toward them are being aroused. Talk about making objects of people.

It's as if feminism, in its effort to win respect for women, decided to trade gender roles instead. Women are praised to the extent they act like men, and men are praised for how womanly they become.

Are we willing to do what it takes, to *be* what it takes, to let our boys be boys, and help them grow to be men? *Real* men? Or will we sit back and take the long, sloping pathway to a gender-neutral, unisex future for our sons?

Let's commit ourselves to doing the extra laundry and living with the noise, if that's what it takes to save the males for our children and grandchildren's generations.

Manly Virtues

The reason boys give us trouble comes from the untrained, uncontrollable masculine characteristics they carry. God did not create an Adam and Anti-Adam, or an Eve and Eve Prime; He created two complementary beings that together reflect the image of God in their humanity. Neither one can display God's image as well individually as the two can together. God gave certain manly tendencies to the man, and womanly tendencies to the woman.

It ought to be obvious that we are interfering with the design if we try to bend one half of it to look more like the other. Maybe we can force it, distort part of it sufficiently, that we can impress a more womanly character on the man, or vice versa, but we are twisting the framework and losing the distinct contribution of whichever half is distorted.

Instead, let's try to retain the character that God intended. Let's proceed in the belief that our boys are built to be manly, but they're just young and untaught. Their behavior may be hard to control (by Mom and Dad) because the young men don't know how to control it themselves yet. They need training, teaching, discipleship—the same as all children need instruction in everything necessary to be rightly-functioning adults. And the persons who train them need to have a sympathetic understanding of just what they're made of.

The first part of this book is a look at some of the masculine characteristics or tendencies which are present in all of our sons. These are meant to ripen into the manly virtues of the adult male when they've been properly understood, disciplined, cultivated, and practiced.

And what are the manly virtues?

In many cases, they're the same things we complain about in our boys: competitiveness, aggression, a desire for adventure (commonly called recklessness?). We may admire the independent spirit of a man but grind our teeth when exhibited by our son. How about messy, scary ideas like heroism, courage, endurance, fortitude? Real men should be protectors, persistent, honorable, intrepid. There's precious little that's neat and nothing that's quiet about those things.

Those virtues are present in seed form in our boys. Will we cultivate them and help bring them to fruition? Or will we trade the opportunity for a little more peace and quiet, and hope their future will take care of itself?

1

SOMEONE TO LOOK UP TO

The North Carolina coast is a complex thing, with a ring of barrier islands, shoals, and sandbars guarding huge sounds and a wandering estuary region. It has been a haven for smugglers, blockade runners, and desperate men as long as history records. It is a wild place that even today can't be fully patrolled or secured, and it is a romantic spot, a place of adventure, full of mysterious and colorful characters.

Unfortunately, many of them are dark characters.

North Carolina was home base for the infamous Edward Teach, known as Blackbeard, and numerous other pirates of the 17th and 18th centuries. There is some fascinating underwater archeology going on right now, and we recently toured the labs at East Carolina University where artifacts from Blackbeard's vessel, *Queen Anne's Revenge*, are being classified and preserved. Anything dredged up from a shipwreck draws our attention and objects associated with the famous pirate's career are especially interesting.

The state history museum recently featured these items in an exhibit about the pirate history of our coast, and chose the highly regrettable name "Knights of the Black Flag" as its title. The radio spots promoting the exhibit finished with a school boy stating how he wanted to be a knight of the black flag, too.

How sad. A young man sees a historic exhibit and is inspired to associate himself with thieves, brigands, and murderers. Our tax dollars at work, folks. Surely we can do better than this at home. Indeed, we *must*.

Boys need heroes

Men and the boys who become them have a need for respect, but they are ready to give it as well. Boys really like having someone they can look up to, someone to admire, someone to claim as their hero. The recent wars in the Middle East have produced hundreds of real, live, hometown heroes. Aside from them, though, the attention and adulation of our sons gravitates toward great athletes, grimly masculine actors, and angst-ridden fictional characters like Batman or Spiderman. The media is pervasive with this kind of hero, and often our own example of those we admire tends that way as well.

What we admire, we tend to become. Are these the men we wish our boys to be like? Or do our sons have more worthy role models in their lives, men they can truly emulate to the glory of God as well as their own benefit? Boys learn so much by example, observation and role-playing, we need to make sure they have the right kind of patterns for them to follow, to judge their actions by, to think about. It's our privilege to help them locate those worthwhile heroes.

What is a hero?

When we speak of a hero, we mean simply a role model whose accomplishments and character are worthy of respect. They may be mighty warriors, selfless missionaries, talented surgeons, or gifted scholars. They may even be really phenomenal baseball players. What we desire in heroes is men we can point out to our sons and say, "Strive to be like him."

We have to be balanced in this, because we're dealing with fallen man; the best of us still grapple with sin in our lives, and some men rise to prominence with scandal clinging to their coat-tails. Francis Schaeffer said that art can be technically well done or it can be poorly executed, and it can accurately express a Biblical truth or it can promote an ungodly worldview. We should strive to produce and support good art with a good message, and nothing else. Likewise, we need to direct our sons to role models which have both skill *and* character.

Recently we watched the movie *Patton* with our older sons. The latter half of the film is a classical tragedy; the gifted leader and tactician at the peak of his success is brought low by his pride and inability to control his tongue. We explain to our sons that because General Patton overcame personal difficulties — he was severely dyslexic — and invested tremendous effort, self-discipline, and courage to become one of America's greatest generals, his accomplishments have earned our respect and can serve as a good example *in those areas.* However, his legendary profanity and his insubordinate behavior toward higher command ultimately destroyed his career, and these character issues make him unsuitable as a role model.

Theodore Roosevelt likewise overcame near-crippling childhood asthma by grit, determination, and a tremendous amount of exercise. His capacity for work and drive for excellence gave him success in several careers, a Nobel Prize and the Congressional Medal of Honor, and even as president he was famous as a family man and church member. While we might not agree with his highly autonomous view of the presidency's powers, we can praise his accomplishments *and* his character and recommend him highly to our sons.

What does the Bible say about heroes?

The older translations of the Bible never use the word "hero;" it appears in some of the recent ones, but more frequently the same term is translated "mighty man." What does appear, and often, is the expectation that young men will learn by following noble, mighty, and godly exemplars.

Accordingly, the Bible is full of examples of admirable men. Even the youngest child in a Christian family can start a list—David slaying the giant, Samson wreaking vengeance on the Philistines, Moses unleashing God's plagues on Egypt then parting the Red Sea on the way out.

It's not just men of war who are held up as a pattern. Men of faith are often men of valor as well, like the Babylonian exiles, Daniel, Shadrach, Meshach, and Abednego. What did Paul undergo for the sake of preaching the Gospel? He gives a partial list:

> From the Jews five times I received forty stripes minus one. Three times I was beaten with rods; once I was stoned; three times I was shipwrecked; a night and a day I have been in the deep; in journeys often, in perils of waters, in perils of robbers, in perils of my own countrymen, in perils of Gentiles, in perils in the city, in perils in the wilderness, in perils in the sea, in perils among false brethren; in weariness and toil, in sleepless-ness often, in hunger and trial, in fastings often, in cold and nakedness—[1]

Only death ended his activity, and through his writing, even the executioner's sword failed to silence him. And Paul told the church in Corinth, "I urge you, imitate me ... Imitate me, just as I also imitate Christ."[2]

The Bible gives examples of false heroes, too. Some are mighty in deed but serve the wrong cause: Goliath, for example, was a hero of the Philistines, and the Moabites had "lion-like" heroes (who, by the way, were vanquished by one of King David's *second-string* "mighty men," Benaiah).[3]

More pernicious are those whose activities can't even be praised on their own merits. Goliath at least was an awesome warrior, and you could admire his prowess in battle apart from his false religion. Men who desecrate the whole idea of heroism are worse. Isaiah declares woe against men who are "heroes in drinking wine, and valiant men in mixing strong drink." Some heroism.[4]

And when the Lord declares judgment on Jerusalem and Judah, He says He will take away "the hero and the warrior."[5] We need our heroes.

The First and the Ultimate

The boy's first hero should definitely be his dad. He is the first adult male figure the baby recognizes and he will inevitably be an example for him — a good example to emulate or a bad one to react to. That is a real challenge for us as fathers. Someone said that a child's first ideas about God come from ideas about his father. Will he be strong, loving, protecting, or frightening, distant, or absent? What a humbling thought that our little sons will form impressions about God's love, God's power, God's provision from our acts of love and power and provision as fathers. This should call us to strive to imitate Christ in a whole new way so that our sons can see Christ in us.

As he grows, though, the boy's ultimate hero should be Christ; Dad should point the way, and like Paul, challenge his son to

follow his father's example as closely (and *only*) as dad is following Christ. The Lord Jesus should be held up before our sons at
every opportunity as the ultimate example of a man: strong, yet
gentle; holy, yet forgiving; avoiding sin; serving others without
self-concern; laying down His life for His brethren.

We should be careful to teach the full character of Christ. Everyone has seen the Sunday school pictures of Jesus, with long,
sleek hair, carrying lambs or gently blessing the children or tapping lightly on the door representing man's heart. Modernity has
banished the Medieval woodcuts of Martin Luther's day, where
Christ is exalted on a throne of judgment, casting the wicked to
their well-deserved destruction. Teach your sons that Christ is
gentle with His people, but that He is also given "a sharp sword,
that with it He should strike the nations." [6]

Too often, Christ is presented to boys as an unimpressive,
feeble, almost effeminate character, unworthy of admiration as
the Savior of mankind and the conqueror of death. Better, for
our sons, the vision in *The Dream of The Rood*, an eighth century
verse where the Anglo-Saxon poet relates the crucifixion from
the perspective of the wooden Cross:

> *Then the young Hero laid His garments by,*
> *He that was God Almighty, strong and brave;*
> *And boldly in the sight of all He mounted*
> *The lofty cross, for He would free mankind.*
> *Then, as the Man divine clasped me, I shook;*
> *Yet dared I not bow to the earth nor fall*
> *Upon the ground, but I must needs stand fast.*
> *A cross upraised, I lifted a great King,*
> *Lifted the Lord of heaven; and dared not bow.*[7]

Jesus is no victim; He is a hero, a mighty king, who boldly embraces the Cross to redeem His people from sin and death and Satan himself. Now *that's* a real man.

Heroes between "first" and "ultimate"

Between the first and the ultimate, there are many smaller heroes that influence our boys' characters. This is where we need to stop and think through what we're doing. If our sons are watching smart-mouth comedies on television, exploring the dark side of comic book heroes at the theater, and reading cynical children's novels, what kind of heroes are they setting up for themselves?

This is where a boy needs his parents. His tastes are unformed and just like with food, what seems most appealing on the surface is often not nutritious at all. If you wouldn't serve your son candy and ice cream at every meal, the diet for his mind and soul shouldn't be exclusively candy, either. We don't object to books and shows and music that are just fun with no real literary or artistic value — Hal calls them "potato chips of the mind" — , but we try to keep them in the same proportion as candy and soft drinks in a good diet — occasional treats, not staples.

Visual media

Television and movies are a critical area because men tend to be very visual. Melanie has noticed when visiting a relative's house where the TV is on, she has to practically stand in front of the set and shout to get the boys' (and the men's) attention. The moving images on the screen absorb their attention in a remarkable way. Because of this, we need to be very careful what our sons put into their minds through visual media. She often tells our sons how she saw a commercial for a horror movie when she was 12 years old and still gets the willies when she remembers it today. Research seems to indicate that what we put in our mind stays there forever; that even if we seemingly forget an image, it remains there to be triggered one day by the right stimulus. Why in the world would we give Satan ammunition that can be used against us for decades?

We decided when our second son was born that we would cancel our cable TV. It seemed like we had so much to do that was important and we were spending so much time watching worthless programs because they filled the half hour between the "good" ones, it just made sense to get rid of it altogether. After a few weeks of withdrawal from round-the-clock news availability, we found we got along quite well without it.

After several months without TV at home, we went on a trip and stayed at a motel. We were so excited to be able to watch TV again for a little while — until we turned it on. We were shocked at what we saw! "What had happened to our culture in those few short months?" was our first thought. Suddenly we realized that nothing had changed but us. Our consciences had been seared by constant exposure to violence, immorality, dazzle and shock. Once we were not exposed to it for a time, we were suddenly able to see it for what it is.

That experience made us decide we would not be a family that kept the TV on all the time. In fact, we never subscribed to cable again and don't even try to pick up broadcast stations. We have seldom missed it, and the Internet has made news available when instant updates are needed (like tracking approaching hurricanes). Isn't it better for our children to live out their own adventures than spend their lives watching other people who are pretending to have a life for the cameras? How pathetic.

We do enjoy movies and some old television shows, so we do have a TV set up with a DVD and VCR player, and sometimes we watch old television programs downloaded from the Internet. Some of those are just fluff—the candy we spoke of earlier. Others, though fun, relaxing entertainment, do provide those heroes our sons can learn from. Old Roy Rogers movies are a great example. Roy, though not a perfect hero, always defends the weak, fights evil, and stands for what is right in a remarkably wholesome way. The songs are great, too.

Old movies like *Mr. Smith goes to Washington* or *It's A Wonderful Life* give our sons an example of men who stand against corruption and greed no matter what it costs. The growing independent Christian film movement is producing more good films every year that we can use to put proper heroes in front of our sons.

Like unfettered TV, the parent-controlled videos can become habit forming too, so we have to watch ourselves to guard against substituting fifteen hours of good clean potato chips for fifteen hours of stupid and cynical potato chips. Overall, the problem is not the medium, it's the message—and the trade off in time and opportunity—that has to be monitored.

Dealing with mixed content in film and TV

There are a lot of films and shows—well, plays, operas, music, paintings, and books, too—that offer some wonderful heroes or great lessons, but have elements that are unsuitable for immature viewers. Some of these are great art, as Francis Schaeffer described them, but have the mark of our besetting sins and faulty world views that tarnish some elements. Do we discard them for a certain level of bad words or disturbing images, or is there some artistic merit that overrides or balances our discomfort or distaste?

We have to exercise discretion here. Some works may be appropriate for older sons, and may be important for their understanding of human philosophy and secular thought so they can learn to counter falsehood with truth, but may be too intense for younger sons. There may be images that lead your sons to sin, or language that is just inappropriate for anyone to repeat.

There are a number of ways we've dealt with this. The most straightforward approach is to remember that the First Amendment applies to the government, not our living room. The author or filmmaker doesn't have *any* right to say just *anything* in our home, simply because we invited his work in. We have cheerfully removed a page from a book, or covered over an illustration, or even blacked out profanity from books which are otherwise acceptable or even useful. There are software or hardware packages that will drop out the occasional curse in a video movie. Call it censorship if you like, but we're raising eternal souls here, not hard-line civil libertarians.

There may be a time to cull the parents' collection, too. Both of us have discarded or sold books and other media that may have been acceptable for college students and single adults, but were simply too much to have around young, precocious readers. Maybe some can be put into storage or loaned to a friend for a few years, until the family has grown into them. It is amazing what even "nice" kids will find tempting, and we shouldn't cling to possessions that are becoming snares to our sons' souls.

Movies and television are harder to edit. If there are images that could lead your sons to sin or be too disturbing, then you may need to give the movie a miss, fast forward past certain segments — there are scenes of *The Lord of the Rings* I still haven't seen — or if your sons are of a discerning age, train them (and yourselves) to avert their eyes. This is useful in the checkout line, too. Do we really *care* how much weight the leading starlet gained when her tough guy actor-friend dumped her for a different bikini model? Should we, Christian?

On the other hand, if there are themes that teach the wrong thing, or a protagonist who doesn't do the right thing, it can be a wonderful teaching opportunity. Whenever we watch a film as a family, we always have a discussion afterward (and sometimes during — other people may not like to watch a movie with us at home). The first question is always, "What is the theme?" Now, don't panic if you don't remember a thing from your last literature course. Theme is the essential lesson the work is teaching, the underlying message. For example, if we're watching *The Incredibles* and the boys answer, "It's about a superhero family that fights a really mean guy," you counter, "No, that's the topic. I'm trying to find out what the theme is — what is the message the director and screenwriter are trying to teach you?" Keep talking until someone in the family figures out the actual theme — in this example, that you should use the talents you have been given to fulfill your mission in life, not be discontented and try to be something you are not. In *Spiderman*, the theme is stated outright — with great power comes great responsibility.

Once you all understand the theme, then talk about how the director and screenwriter are teaching that theme through the plot, the characters, the setting, the music and the cinematography. When your children understand how their emotions and judgment can be influenced by what the director chooses to film in dark scenes versus light scenes, the symbolism of the background, or what kind of music is playing during the scene, they will no longer be carried along by the sweeping experience — they will be learning to pick out the message in anything they see or hear and understand how that message is conveyed and people are influenced. This will help them gain the discernment they need to resist being led astray by the world. It will be a huge protection for them and will also teach them how to communicate truth more effectively.

Heroes from history

People who meet our family are often intrigued by our sons' names. Most know them by their shortened versions, but when we introduce them, we make a point of saying this is John Calvin, Caleb McLeod, Matthew Henry, Samuel Adams, Seth Harral, and David Brainerd.[8] They're like a calling card, in some ways; anyone versed in church history could guess our theological bent, including as they do a Swiss reformer, a Presbyterian Bible commentator, a Puritan patriot, and a Congregational missionary to the Indians (Caleb and Seth have family names that we wanted to preserve). By giving them names of historic significance, we have given our sons an immediate legacy to live up to. Maybe it's a bit of the "patron saint" effect.

Another activity we've found useful is researching family history. Hal's father, who was an only child, made an effort to document everything he could find about the Youngs; Hal spent many Saturday afternoons sitting beside his father in the microfilm rooms at county courthouses and archives, copying census reports and tax records. His father died many years ago, and the files sat undisturbed until Melanie's mother revived Hal's interest in the subject. In the meanwhile, the Internet had revolutionized genealogy and put millions of pages of historical records at our fingertips. Hal delved back into the study, discovering not only a world of newly accessible information, but his dad's files — with Hal's own notes, taken in self-conscious fifth grader's cursive. With a mild start, he realized he was the same age, exactly, as his father had been at that time.

In the past several years, Hal has been able to reconstruct a great deal of our family history on both his and Melanie's side. He has found military records of ancestors who fought in the Revolution and the Civil War, church histories that mention clergymen in the family tree, details about the marriages, family life, community involvement and daily activity of hundreds of the boys' forefathers. It has become a bit of a joke with our local homeschool history club, where the leaders will announce the topic of the meeting and turn to the boys with the question, "Did the Youngs have ancestors involved in this incident?" ("Well, actually ... " they usually begin).

There were few men in our family tree that history would call "great;" most were just soldiers in the ranks, farmers and merchants, pastors in country chapels, just average people. At the same time, we have been able to challenge the boys to remember their heritage — young couples who braved the Atlantic crossing in the 1600's, the men who stayed to surrender with their units at Appomattox rather than desert with their neighbors, the pastors and editors who stood fast in the face of controversy, and the laymen who helped build new churches and communities. Most of our sons will never be called to raise a flag over some future Iwo Jima, but they will all be called to be faithful in the daily battles of the Christian walk. Each of our families has examples to follow, as well as those to be wary of.

Books are a great source of good heroes for your sons to look up to. Biographies of great leaders and great Christians have influenced many people over the years. Collections of short missionary biographies can give your younger boys a taste for missionary heroism and show them it's not the sinners that have the best adventures. Longer biographies and narratives will teach the older boys how the Lord's servants face opposition but triumph through His grace; classic studies of men like William Carey, David Livingston, John Paton, and Adoniram Judson give incredible accounts of these men's fights with life-threatening opposition, temptation, and despair, to finally see God's word implanted in hearts.

Don't overlook the value of secular biographies either. The lives of men like Patrick Henry, Winston Churchill, Thomas Edison, Booker T. Washington, and Theodore Roosevelt give great examples of perseverance in the face of discouragement, overcoming difficulty against all odds, and standing with integrity and character that gains the victory in their fields. Popular biographies on the adult market, like David McCollough's *John Adams* or Joseph J. Ellis' *His Excellency, George Washington*, are great recommendations for older sons and can be excerpted for reading aloud. There are numerous excellent series of short biographies, now being reprinted, under the *Discovery, Childhood of Famous Americans,* and *Landmark* series.

What about heroes from modern times, men who are still alive and often still active in their fields? The same principles apply — we have to look at accomplishment and character, with an added caution that all of us are prone to sin, and while we live, history does not have time to bring every detail of our lives to the light. Many prominent men, whether leaders in politics, religion, or any other field, have embarrassing or scandalous secrets carefully protected in their personal lives. We may find admirable traits in their character and achievement, but we have to remind our sons that only God knows the hearts of men, and we must not be surprised when celebrated persons fall from a great height.

Fictional characters

There's a place for fiction in Christian life; Jesus and the prophets taught in parables and allegories, so we do not need to shun them ourselves. Often a fictionalized character or situation can be more powerful and less ambiguous to teach a principle to our sons.

For younger boys, we've found classics like Edna Walker Chandler's "Cowboy Sam" series will hold their attention and provide adventure and character in equal measure. And how many people have heard the radio dramatizations of "The Sugar Creek Gang"? Paul Hutchens based his series of 36 books on the adventures he had growing up in rural Indiana with his six brothers.[9] Each of these books feature likeable characters who grow and develop as they face challenges to their strength, courage, honesty and faith.

Finding good fiction for older sons can be something of a challenge, and we tend to recommend older classics. *The Swiss Family Robinson* is a family favorite — we've read the covers off two copies — if you can overlook the admittedly strange mix of geography and wildlife that appears. *Robinson Crusoe* and *Pilgrim's Progress* are excellent reading for individuals or family. All three of these had strong Christian messages in the original versions; modern editions of *Crusoe* and *Robinson* sometimes omit this, so it is worth looking for unabridged versions. Charles Sheldon's classic *In His Steps* gave rise to the "WWJD" marketing wave several years ago, but the book is a solid challenge to put feet on our faith.

The historical novels by G. A. Henty and adventure stories by R. M. Ballantyne are late Victorian-era books, intended for young teens but written with a vocabulary that modern college students may find challenging. The main characters are young men who are believers or come to faith in the course of their interaction with real historic events and places. Many of these are available in recorded format, which can be an encouragement to younger sons or can be useful on long trips in the van.

While her protagonists are usually female, Grace Livingston Hill wrote a few of her novels with a young man or a father in the central role. *The Prodigal Girl* follows a father's attempt to reclaim his family, especially his teen-aged daughter, from their slide into the temptations of a prosperous but spiritually dead lifestyle; they eventually end up homeschooling, a remarkable suggestion when it was written in the 1920s. Better still is *The Witness*, the story of a college student who is challenged by the testimony and courageous death of a classmate to re-examine his own claim to Christianity, and how he is nearly led astray by a clever but devious young woman.

Unfortunately, we have not found many modern works of fiction to recommend for older sons that present good heroes. By that time, we generally are moving them toward history and biography to find good examples in reading. And by all means, though they no longer need you to read *to* them, keep reading *with* them and discussing what you find.

Conclusion

Our sons learn by examples — ours, and those of role models around them. They need heroes to follow, and they will find them one place or another. Will they form their view of masculinity from secular media and entertainment, from the athletic field, from the music industry or from youth culture? Or will they have parents who take the time to give them positive examples of righteous manliness from their own family, from the pages of Scripture and history, and even from the world of fiction and the imagination? Will their heroes show them how to face temptation and stand strongly in the face of adversity, or will we allow them to embrace a culture of hedonism and materialism that only saps the spirit and leaves them cynical, ironic, and passive? Will they naturally ask themselves, "What would Jesus do in this situation? What would Dad do? What would Martin Luther, or Samuel Adams, or William Wilberforce, or Orville Wright do? Would they surrender, prevaricate, compromise, quit? Or is there a better way to follow?"

They *will* have heroes. For their own sakes, make sure they're the right ones.

NOTES ON CHAPTER 1

[1] 2 Corinthians 11:24-27

[2] 1 Corinthians 4:16, 11:1

[3] 2 Samuel 23:20

[4] Isaiah 5:22 (NASB)

[5] Isaiah 3:2 (NIV)

[6] Revelation 19:15

[7] *The Dream of the Rood,* lines 39-45. Translated by Lamotte Iddings in *Select Translations From Old English Poetry,* Albert S. Cook and Chauncey B. Tinker, eds. (New York: Ginn & Co., 1902), pp. 93-99. Accessed on Google Books, 22 June 2009.

[8] Our daughters are Susannah Ruth, whose name follows several women on both sides of the family, and Katherine Luther, named after the former nun who became Martin Luther's wife, whom he affectionately called his "rib."

[9] There is a "New Sugar Creek Gang" series which we are not as enthusiastic about, since it has introduced more girls and modern problems and situations into the story line.

2

Is There Not A Cause?

Have you added a brand new driver to your auto insurance recently? No? Brace yourself.

We've added two in the past few years and will probably add another two before they start graduating to financial independence. They're boys, too, and that's the biggest increase of all. The insurance business, after all, is a game of statistics, and groups which have a high claims history get their rates boosted. Young men are high risk customers, and why? Probably because they don't have a strong grasp of their own mortality. They *like* risks; they like adrenaline; they love adventure and powerful machines and fast travel. Couple that with a mix of inexperience and braggadocio and you've got a real storm brewing. The question may not be "Why do so many young men wreck their cars?" but rather, "How do *any* of them make it home?"

A few years ago John Eldredge's book *Wild At Heart* became a bestseller. Part of his premise is that men should not be tamed or domesticated but should actively pursue adventure. It affirms their God-given nature to be out in the wilderness, fighting with nature, fear, the elements. Strip them of the opportunity and something of their manhood goes awry.

There is a world of different ways this can be expressed and not just by outdoor activities. The relentless pursuit of an elusive goal can play out in the marketplace, the laboratory, the studio, the prayer closet. Often the spectacular success goes to the man who follows Napoleon's dictum of "Audacity, always audacity!"

Young men have a tremendous desire to try their strength and to be tested in return. This is integral to their competitive nature, but let's take a look at how it impacts their interaction with the real world, not the contrived world of competitions.

A Biblical view of adventure and recklessness

Adults sometimes equate a desire for adventure with immaturity and recklessness. The Bible makes a distinction and so should we. The desire to conquer, to win against the odds, to do great things — these can be admirable ambitions. The willingness to pit one's nerve against an unsettling foe is frequently called for in Scripture: *Have I not commanded you? Be strong and of good courage,* is repeated six times to Joshua and Israel before initiating the conquest of Canaan.[1] The same phrase appears in passages calling for moral courage to carry out God's commandments or to undertake a major project (the building of the Temple!).[2] The righteous man is *bold as a lion,* and God gives His people boldness to preach the Gospel.[3] Paul — and all the churches of the Gentiles — say thanks to Aquila and Priscilla, *"who risked their own necks for my life."* [4]

On the other hand, overconfidence and rashness is soundly criticized. The Proverbs say, "He who is *impulsive exalts folly...he sins who hastens with his feet."* [5] When Satan tempted Jesus to presume on God's protection, Christ rebuked him:

> Then the devil took Him up into the holy city, set Him on
> the pinnacle of the temple, and said to Him, "If You are
> the Son of God, throw Yourself down. For it is written:

'He shall give His angels charge over you,' *and,* 'In their hands they shall bear you up,/Lest you dash your foot against a stone.'"

Jesus said to him, "It is written again, 'You shall not tempt the LORD your God.'"[6]

The sin of presumption takes many forms, whether denying what God has clearly revealed, or attempting to test His patience and provision. The reckless man may be doing both; the one who is serving Him may be guilty of neither.

Bring on the boldness

Without that adventurous spirit, there wouldn't be many discoveries or inventions; few great soldiers; no great explorers. The question for us as parents is how to channel a God-given desire for adventure into productive, God-honoring endeavors, rather than let it slide into pointless, potentially self-destructive recklessness. Can we send them off with a cheer, or must it be with fear?

There's no question that child-rearing has changed over the past several decades. The boys in *The Sugar Creek Gang* had a freedom to roam and explore that is seldom seen today — they wander around the countryside, swim in the creeks, fish and hunt and camp. These books were published between 1939 and 1972 but were inspired by an earlier era. Books from even earlier times show boys treated as young men — they join ships' crews, leave on expeditions, and undertake other adventures and trials at an age modern culture considers mid-childhood.

Today's youth are barely considered able to look after themselves before they're old enough to vote. A local television station's website recently held a story about a crisis which happened under a babysitter's care. The majority of the reader comments which followed suggested that children should not be left alone ever, much less in charge of other children, until they were close to eighteen.

What's changed? Society has shifted its focus.

There's a God-given drive to take care of the physical needs of children; a crying baby *cannot* be ignored. In the so-called Christian world, we've also protected them spiritually, controlling what influences they were exposed to and making sure they were taught right and wrong. We understood some things were inappropriate for children. And we understood to varying degrees that eternity trumped everything—there are some things that are just more important that what we see here.

Now that we live in a post-Christian culture, though, new issues come to the fore. There is no longer much emphasis on children's spiritual health. The educational system which once had a broad tolerance toward basic Christian teaching is now officially agnostic, though it is, in fact, skeptical or hostile toward Christianity. Religion has given way to "values," which can be redesigned as needed to conform to popular trends. The UN Treaty on the Rights of the Child even insists that children have the right to be exposed to whatever media they wish. Statistics on the relatively low percentage of students enrolled in Christian schools suggests this hasn't risen to a universal level of concern for many Christian parents. Without the spiritual concern, only the physical remains.

As a result, fewer people have the hope of heaven. If you don't believe in life after death, then protecting your own life and the lives of those you love becomes paramount. It is literally all you have. When you have assurance of eternal life in Christ, you know there are more important things than physical existence.

Without question, we have an absolute responsibility to give our children physical protection; they are dependent on our care to provide their food, clothing and shelter, and to shield them from those who would exploit or abuse them in some way.

That protection shouldn't become the unmanning of our sons, though. Boys need to have the freedom to take reasonable risks. You don't let them play in traffic, but you shouldn't cringe in horror as they climb the jungle gym. If they grow up fearful of risk, they are missing an important part of being a man. A carefully considered risk, prayerfully undertaken, is not recklessness.

The recklessness we see is an expression of a child's natural foolishness. In our country, the artificial age range of adolescence continues to rise, where college students and even college graduates are given a pass for remarkably irresponsible behavior. Young boys disobey their parents and break things; young men drive too fast and have accidents, and as they grow older, the potential consequences get worse and worse.

But C.S. Lewis wrote in *Mere Christianity* that temptations and sins are sometimes "the excess or perversion" of godly traits.[7] Reckless behavior, particularly in young boys, may be the uncontrolled expression of a legitimate, even godly, desire to strive after great and noble deeds. And when the desire for adventure follows a God-honoring course, exciting things can happen: cannibals are converted to Christ, children are plucked from burning ships, great discoveries are made, businesses are created, Bibles appear in closed countries.

So how can we distinguish between the two, and direct our sons to the better way?

Adventure in the Cause of Christ

We can start by teaching our sons that the Christian life, lived out in practical application, is not a meek and retiring sort of thing, blinking behind thick round glasses. This is where they find heroes — in the biographies of strong, active, courageous men who lived for Christ — some as missionaries, evangelists and reformers, certainly, but some in other fields. When they learn of the incredible adventures of David Livingstone, find out how Robert E. Lee and Joshua Chamberlain applied Christianity to military service, read of the bravery of Richard Wurmbrand, and imagine themselves taking Bibles to Communist countries with "God's Smuggler", they will begin to understand that it takes a real man to be a real Christian man. When they understand that Christianity offers not only a way of life but something worth dying for, they may also realize the foolishness of risking death for nothing.

Hal ran into an acquaintance from high school his first few weeks of college. The two had only been in a couple of classes together so they weren't very close, but there were few from home at this college and it was good to see someone you already knew. The other freshman was on crutches, nursing a leg in a cast, so naturally Hal asked what happened.

"Oh, I broke my ankle skydiving last weekend," he said, adding brightly, "I've been nominated to be president of the skydiving club."

Within the year, he was dead in another skydiving accident.

We're not certain what this young man was pursuing; he may have aspired to become a military paratrooper or Forest Service smoke jumper and hoped to accelerate his training by learning the basic skill as a civilian parachutist. But it does raise the question: Was he just seeking a thrill?

Our boys should be active and adventurous, but careful of themselves at the ultimate extreme, understanding that life is a gift and their bodies are the temple of the Holy Spirit. To risk life meaninglessly is foolishness; note that God's gifts of boldness and courage are not for self-fulfillment or entertainment but for greater service to Him. Our sons can go skydiving for kicks or they can join the Army and protect our country with those same skills. They can stay out late bar-crawling and club-hopping in a big city, or they can go with a missionary to a foreign city in a closed country. They can hack computer networks and vandalize websites for fun, or they can use the same knowledge to set up Christian sites to evade a tyrannical country's censors. Which is really more exciting? Which is vanity and a striving after wind?

When to Comfort, When to Encourage

Once they grasp this principle, we need to look for opportunities for them to take reasonable and productive risks. It is very important at this point, that when sons begin to step out that mothers don't undermine them. When a son says, "Mama, I am really afraid of making that speech in front of all those people," it is very tempting for a nurturing mom to say, "Oh, Honey, I so want this to be a good experience for you. I don't blame you for being scared. I would be, too. Why don't we just cancel?" Comforting feeds our natural tendencies and we don't have to find clean clothes for everyone so we can go. Unfortunately, instead of the affirming sympathy Mom intended, sometimes boys hear this as, "I didn't think you could do it. It's really too hard for you."

A much better response would be, "Son, it's not unusual to get butterflies a bit before you speak in public, I often feel the same way. You just pray and ask the Lord for help and do it anyway. Courage doesn't mean you aren't afraid, it means you do what you ought to regardless. I think you have a really good speech and I believe you'll do a great job. Let's go get ready." They really just want to know that you believe in them.

It may be that mothers have a hard time discerning between when sons need comforting and when they need bucking up. Here's a rule of thumb: If he hasn't faced the trial yet, or he's in the midst of it — encourage him. If he's been to the wars and is limping home wounded — comfort him. Once the wounds are bound up, encourage him to rise and face the fight again.

An Age for Risk

Speaking of war, there are two good reasons that young men are called to the fight. Naturally, young men are at their peak strength and stamina in their early twenties — they make good soldiers physically. It's also true, though, that their thirst for adventure and their youthful idealism peak at that same time. They are not only well suited for the challenge of war, but in most cases, they are independent, with no family depending on their return.

What better time to take the considered, God-honoring risk? This is not only a time to serve in the military but an outstanding time to spend a summer with a foreign missionary or work in an inner-city ministry. It's a great time to spend a semester studying abroad or a summer traveling and working in a completely different part of the country. It's a time to take on a major project — to buy a car at auction and restore it for resale or to buy a small house to fix up, when only he would have to live amid the sawdust and bare walls while the remodeling was underway. It's a fantastic time to start a business, when he's old enough to take a man's part in the world, but before he has house payments to meet and a wife and child to live on the shoestring with him. He can become a volunteer fireman, a park ranger, an adult literacy coach, a volunteer of a thousand kinds. He can take risks that endanger little but can really pay off. Let's not let our middle age "sense" dampen his enthusiasm!

Conclusion

An adventure is really anything that involves risk. A careless risk undertaken thoughtlessly or in pursuit of a thrill is recklessness, but a hazard confronted for the glory of God is a different matter altogether. This desire in our sons can be met by teaching them to face their fears head on—by public speaking or by taking on the responsibility of an adult or by learning to swim. It can be fed rappelling down a cliff or walking ten miles or interacting in a foreign language. It certainly includes sharing the gospel—nearly always an adventure. Teach your sons to take good risks, reasonable, godly risks. Teach them to love godly adventure—and stand back and see what God has in mind for them!

NOTES FOR CHAPTER 2

Title: When young David was sent to take provisions to his brothers serving in the army, his older brother Eliab accused him of simply coming to see the battle. David replied, "What have I done now? *Is there* not a cause?" He had good reason to be in an exciting location (see 1 Samuel 17:1-29).

[1] Deuteronomy 31:6, 7, 23; Joshua 1:6, 7, 9 (NASB)

[2] 1 Chronicles 22:13; 28:20 (NASB)

[3] Proverbs 28:1; Acts 4:13, 29, 31

[4] Romans 16:4

[5] Proverbs 14:29; 19:2

[6] Matthew 4:5-7

[7] C.S. Lewis, *Mere Christianity: A revised and amplified edition, with a new introduction* (New York: HarperCollins Publishers, 2001), p. xii.

3

Standing Alone

The negative stereotype of homeschoolers says that boys taught at home will be withdrawn, painfully shy, ill-equipped to deal with challenges of the world outside their home.

Our eldest son, who was homeschooled from the beginning, was handed a wallet full of money and instructed to take a visiting business client he'd just met on a 1300-mile sightseeing trip. He was to serve as guide and interpreter, handling arrangements and addressing any problems with drivers, hotels, and restaurants.

In China. By himself. At the age of 17.

So much for ill-equipped.

The Way it Used to Be

We all expect that our sons will grow to be strong, independent men, able to support themselves and their families, prepared to stand up for their beliefs, able to take on the world if necessary. What we've forgotten, as a culture, is how soon that may be possible.

In 1781, the young John Quincy Adams was sent to Russia as the private secretary of America's diplomatic mission to the court of Catherine the Great. Since the lead diplomat did not speak French, the diplomatic language of Europe, young Adams would be responsible for interpreting discussions and translating any official documents. He was fourteen at the time.

In 1813 midshipman David Farragut, serving aboard the USS *Essex*, was given command of the captured British whaler *Barclay*. Although the English captain of the vessel attempted to take back the ship once they were underway, Farragut faced him down and brought the prize successfully into port. He was twelve years old.

When we first heard stories like this, we were floored. People we knew were amazed that we got married at age 22; "That seems so *young*," they said, though we both had our degrees and Hal was three weeks from commissioning as an Air Force officer. What changed to make the culture go from viewing a 12-year-old as a young adult, to seeing men and women ten years older as barely able to care for themselves?

As we read more about the history of the nation and particularly the changes in its educational system, we realized that young people today are raised with very different expectations than they used to be. We decided that, though we had no idea what the Lord held in store for our sons, we wanted them to be ready to embrace it. We wanted to raise them more like the generation that founded our country.

Getting it All Backwards

Today it is common for young people to have all the freedom of adults to make their own decisions, to choose their entertainment, to have life-changing romantic relationships, and yet to bear none of the responsibilities. They are not expected to support themselves, to suffer the consequences of their sin themselves, to do their work without supervision, to look after themselves. School systems fret that teenagers may make poor choices in the cafeteria line if french fries and soft drinks are available, yet they consider providing family planning services and counseling without the parents' knowledge or consent.

This is backwards from Scripture. The Word says, *"He who is faithful in what is least is faithful also in much,"* [1] so we had a plan: give the boys as much responsibility as they could handle as soon as they were able and give them more as they showed themselves faithful. Here's how:

Responsibility, then Freedom

When it comes to household chores, we try to ask ourselves, "Who is the youngest person who can do this job right now?" Sometimes that'll still mean the oldest. If we're in a hurry or we don't have time to see that it's done right, then the oldest who is home (we call that person, "the senior brother") does it. Often though, we do have plenty of time to supervise and even teach the chore, but don't want to. Too bad. That's our opportunity to go ahead and choose the *youngest* who can do it, or can be helped to do it. This keeps us from leaning too hard on the older ones and making them overwhelmed; it frees these older children up to learn different skills as they mature, and it makes sure the house doesn't fall apart when they go to college or leave home for a few days.

As the boys get older we expect them to come alongside their parents in our ministry opportunities — setting up chairs, babysitting little ones at home — and in our business — marking samples, holding the photo backdrops, cutting fabric swatches, praying. They are a part of all we do, and they are not paid; it's their part of helping to support the family, and building their own inheritance to boot.

Likewise, we try to give the children more and more independence in their school work. We go from constant supervision and checking by Mom, to working independently with occasional checking, to only grading tests and answering questions as needed. That last stage is where we expect our high schoolers to be — not the elementary students ("Help! My seven-year-old doesn't work independently!"). Sometimes we've had children show themselves unfaithful — they skip lessons or do shoddy work as long as they aren't caught. Those children move back a step, for more supervision, more work, more discipline, and the opportunity to do the shoddy work *again*. Those who are faithful, though, are given more responsibility and freedom — to plan their own schedules and to organize their work flow. By the time they graduate, they should be prepared for the independence of college work — though admittedly, for some, this is a much bigger challenge than for others.

Everyone is familiar with the driver's education model: the student learns the basic principles and rules, then it's practice, practice, practice, with close adult supervision. When our boys get their learner's permits, we make them drive under all kinds of situations — interstates at night, country roads, city congestion, wet and icy conditions. Hal has taken them out to a dark, rain-slicked parking lot and had them lock the brakes, so they learn what a skid feels like and how to control it. We've even had them drive through downtown D.C. in rush hour. We want them to encounter everything possible while we're there to instruct, so when they face it on their own, they have confidence and experience though we're not there.

That's our practice in training for independence. We introduce the boys into adult roles, little by little, and help them practice while we can steer the outcome and recover from mistakes.

This can start very early. Melanie begins taking one of the boys with her to the store to carry things and be her protector. A seven-year-old will grow visibly when he's called to be Mama's bodyguard. They love it; there's not much to make a small boy feel manly, but this will. Hal told them years ago that their mother should never be carrying anything until every boy is fully loaded; now they love to take bags out of her arms and tote them into the house.

As they learn to do these things, we let them begin checking out for us in stores. We teach them how to use cash, then the debit card with supervision. Later, we'll begin sending them into small stores while we watch the door for their return (or for distress signals). Eventually, they are able to drive to any store and do any level of shopping without help.

Camps and seminars give boys a chance to stand on their own for a time in situations that are challenging, but still likely to lead to success. We sent a couple of the boys to a challenge camp when they reached age 11 or so. This was an outdoor adventure program that was an enormous physical challenge — rappelling, running obstacle courses, whitewater rafting — and there was a mix of boys in attendance, not just from likeminded families. However, the camp was led by a godly friend of ours who let the boys stay with his family the week of camp. It's a good opportunity to be tested and learn to stand, while knowing that there's a respite at the end of the day and only a week at most to endure.

This kind of controlled entry to interacting with the popular youth culture is an important part of the transition from the Christian home environment to wider adult life in the community. We believe it is difficult for young people to stand against a constant, grinding peer pressure; we've seen it confirm the warnings that *Foolishness is bound up in the heart of a child*, and *the companion of fools will be destroyed.*[2] Our eldest son said one of his biggest disappointments in going to college was seeing how peer dependent his fellow Christian students were. They were even afraid of the opinions of their friends. They seemed more concerned about being "weird" than considering what Christ thought of their actions. Their experiences and fears kept them not only from being bold for Christ; but also kept them from seeking holiness seriously.

We've also gratefully accepted our mothers' invitations to send a boy or two traveling with them, both in the U.S. and overseas. Though they are with an adult, they know she depends on them to help her not just with luggage, but in planning what to do and navigating. That degree of independence when they are out of our household, but still under the care of someone likeminded, is important in allowing them to learn without too much danger.

When our oldest showed himself faithful in these things, we allowed him to fly to San Antonio by himself to attend the San Antonio Independent Christian Film Festival and Academy. He stayed with friends of ours there, but was responsible for himself in traveling and during the day at the Festival. A few summers ago, he took another step. He spent the summer in China working with our brother and business partner. He stayed with a relative who speaks no English and was responsible for taking the subway through the largest city on earth to get to work each day by himself. Although he did not have any likeminded fellowship — my brother is extraordinarily busy and was even out of the country part of the time — he remained faithful: seeking out a church, staying close to the Lord and taking care of himself.

We have had some exceptional opportunities, to be sure, but every family has some way they can teach their sons to be faithfully independent in a step-by-step way. It may be doing jobs on their own, or starting a micro-business, or breeding animals, or planning a wilderness camping trip. It doesn't seem fair to keep sons under constant instruction and supervision, with no chance to stand on their own, then give them complete freedom and responsibility when they come of age. No wonder so many young adults fall into trouble of one kind or another; they need an opportunity to start standing on their own when they don't have to do it very long. Think of it like teaching a baby to walk — first you hold their hands, then you stand just a bit away, then farther away. If they stumble, you can catch them — to a point.

How can you keep them from really hurting themselves when they fall, though?

Avoiding Disaster

Our standard is this — do they have a way of escape from bad influences, and can they handle the responsibility? For example, when we sent our sons to camps of like-minded Christian students, like a worldview program at a nearby campus or an anatomy and physiology camp led by a homeschool father and scientist, we weren't too concerned. For another camp with excellent content — it taught entrepreneurism and business ethics — but a much wider range of students, we were more cautious to find a Christian friend to apply and room with him there. In either case, we've always made sure they were able to call us at any time, as well.

The secret is just what Scripture lays out: A tiny bit of responsibility is given, and when that is handled faithfully, give more. If at any time the child can't handle it, then things are tightened up until they are prepared to try again. Working step by step like that, there is much less chance for disaster.

There's an engineer's joke about how to determine the capacity of a bridge: First you drive a truck across it, then a larger truck, then successively bigger vehicles until the bridge collapses. Then you note the weight of the last truck that crossed, make a sign with that number on it, and rebuild the bridge. It's hard on the truck and hard on the bridge but it does give you a definite answer.

We can't do that with our children, not when the consequences of some failures will change — or end — their lives forever. So how can you let them find their feet to stand alone without courting disaster?

It's through knowing their hearts and understanding where they are spiritually. A young man can't stand alone if he doesn't know God. He can't resist temptation if he is spiritually weak. You have to know. There is no way to do this other than taking the time to really talk to them often. If you don't really know them, you can't hit this careful balance of challenge and growth versus danger and failure.

Learning to Stand

We've had lots of back and forth motion on this path, and we've found you can't expect constant growth in maturity. There are times we have been delighted with a son's progress, only to see them fall flat. Maturity comes like any part of the Christian life — battling through, despite opposition and setback, in baby steps forward and slips backward. We believe, though, that if you consistently strive for your young men to *be* young *men*; if you encourage them to stand for themselves and prepare them to do so; if you are aiming them towards an independent stand for God; you will be amazed at what they become. Our sons are light-years ahead of where we were at those ages — and that's a great thing!

May all our children exceed us in the things that matter — the things of God.

Notes for Chapter 3

[1] Luke 16:10

[2] Proverbs 22:15, 13:20

4

TAKING UP ARMS

There is a popular caricature of the redneck South that invariably includes a pickup truck with a gun rack in the window. You don't see that as much as you once did, for a variety of reasons — for one thing, SUVs have replaced pickup trucks for a lot of men, and a lot more pickups today have extended cabs with extra space behind the seats. You don't need add-on carriers for gear like you once did. Even in our childhood, when the frame of a gun rack was a frequent sight in the trucks around town, most often they were empty or just carried a neatly rolled, black umbrella. After all, in the suburban-to-rural transitional south of the Carolinas where we grew up, men went hunting on the weekends, but they had regular jobs during the week. Maybe a shotgun or rifle was a tool for daily use if you were a rancher out west, but where we called home, they were sports equipment, often passed from father and grandfather to sons and grandsons as cherished heirlooms. Most boys unencumbered with town ordinances had their own BB guns and pellet rifles, graduating to .22 caliber rifles and shotguns when their dads decided they were old enough. And even if you didn't have the real thing, you had your private arsenal of cap pistols and toy weapons of all sorts. It was just boy stuff.

When Hal finished up his military commitment after college — he'd had an ROTC scholarship — his first civilian job was in central California. As parents of a young boy, we made friends easily enough, but learned really quickly that mothers in the Golden State saw guns in a very different light — they didn't allow them, ever, and don't bring any plastic soldiers over to play with, either.

The funny thing was that the restriction, well-intentioned we're sure, didn't seem to keep their sons from seeking the culture of weaponry. The boys nibbled cheese sandwiches into the shape of pistols at lunch. Pieces of scrap wood or broken tree limbs were used as rifles. Somehow the diplomatic approach to crime prevention and international crisis resolution didn't ignite with the boys, who continued playing cowboy or cop or Sergeant Rock, fully armed and loaded, much to their parents' distress.

Back in the South after our "year of exile," as Hal still calls it, we've seen more and more mothers adopting the view that their sons should be protected and kept back from "violent" play. We took some time both in California and in the changing neighborhoods of our native states to look at the issue and come up with a Biblical rationale for it. Should boys be allowed to play with toy weapons, or is this cultivating a taste for violence and mayhem that should be headed off?

Playing is part of the very nature of children. When the Lord returns peace to Zion, elderly people will sit outside and *the city/Shall be full of boys and girls/Playing in its streets.*[1] When Jesus criticized the hard-hearted Jews for rejecting John the Baptist and Himself, He said "*They are like children sitting in the marketplace and calling to one another, saying: 'We played the flute for you,/And you did not dance;/We mourned to you,/And you did not weep.'*"[2] The adults should take their religion seriously enough to consider the message of the prophet and the Messiah. He doesn't fault the children, though, for pretending to hold a celebration or a funeral. That's what children do.

So is the use of force or violence — or the threat to do so — condemned or condoned by Scripture?

Violence and Scripture

There's no question about it in the Old Testament — this is a violent world. God slew an animal to provide Adam and Eve with the first clothing made of skins; He gave His approval to Abel's offering from the flock, which meant the death of those animals; He gave Noah permission to kill animals for food and commanded all kinds of ritual slaughter of animals in the service of the Tabernacle and Temple offerings.[3] God laid out the initial case for capital punishment for the crime of murder early in Genesis and prescribed death as punishment for a number of crimes in ancient Israel.[4] One incident which is exempted from guilt is that of a homeowner using deadly force to protect his family against a burglary or home invasion.

This doesn't even begin to touch the conquest of Canaan, where whole cities were so far down a road of wickedness that God ordered Israel to completely eradicate them.

Does the New Testament change this? Jesus said, "*I tell you not to resist an evil person. But whoever slaps you on your right cheek, turn the other to him also.*"[5] He rebuked Peter for drawing the sword to defend Him from arrest, saying, "*Put your sword in its place, for all who take the sword will perish by the sword.*"[6] Surely the life of Christ has brought the time for nonviolence by believers?

We don't think that's the whole story. While a Christian should be patient under persecution and should not make a lifestyle of pursuing violence for private reasons, Jesus is referring to personal conduct concerning personal matters. We have to remember, too, that Jesus was consumed with zeal for His Father's house and chased the money changers out of the Temple with a whip, looking a little less than meek and mild at that moment.[7] When John the Baptist was approached by soldiers, he did not rebuke them for their military careers, but told them to go about their duties honestly.[8] When a centurion of the Roman occupation forces sent to Jesus to heal his servant, Jesus held up the faith of this Gentile as an example to the Jews.[9] And before leading His disciples into a nighttime confrontation where violence could easily spread beyond its intended victim, Jesus told them to arm themselves: *"he who has no sword, let him sell his garment and buy one."*[10] It seems the use of weapons and force by believers is not ruled out by the Gospels.

Nor is it shunned in the Epistles. Paul used military duty as an example of fortitude to Timothy, commended Epaphroditus and Archippus as *"fellow soldiers,"* and of course wrote the familiar passage of *"the whole armor of God,"* including the sword of the Spirit.[11] The imagery would be hard to explain if the idea of military service and its associated weaponry were off limits for believers.

Even more directly, Paul makes it clear that civil government is given the power of force as an instrument of God's will on earth:

> *For rulers are not a terror to good works, but to evil. Do you want to be unafraid of the authority? Do what is good, and you will have praise from the same. For he is God's minister to you for good. But if you do evil, be afraid;* **for he does not bear the sword in vain; for he is God's minister, an avenger to execute wrath on him who practices evil.** [emphasis added] [12]

The civil authorities — which in this case were the pagan Romans — have God's direction to wield the sword as an instrument of punishment against evildoers. While this passage implies the use of capital punishment, it is a very short step to apply it to the use of weapons by law enforcement officers as well. Since Paul writes elsewhere that believers will sit in judgment over angels and the world, and are therefore qualified to sit as human magistrates here and now,[13] it is no great stretch to conclude that a Christian may be given the same responsibility to bear the sword in a civil role.

So we see the Bible supporting the use of weapons and force in a number of situations. Some depend on the existence of a proper civil authority, such as military service, law enforcement and criminal justice. Personal uses include hunting animals for food or other purposes, or in the extreme situation of self-defense or protection of one's family. Christ's admonition to endure personal insult without retribution does not apply to every situation — particularly when our choice of non-resistance removes protection from those who require our protection. There is no allowance for using force in personal vendetta and revenge, vigilante justice, or to rape and plunder. Even accidental manslaughter carries a penalty.[14]

The problem, you see, is not guns themselves; the problem is the people wielding them. School shootings at Columbine High School and Virginia Tech were not perpetrated by weapons that somehow seized control of their owners and sent them on a rampage. Our sons may very well be called to serve in an armed profession some day, or may need to use weapons to provide for their families or protect them from harm. Why not teach them to respect the power of weapons and handle them properly, the same as we teach them to handle a lawn mower or a power saw, or a sharp knife or boiling water in the kitchen, for that matter, rather than shrink from them as if they were embodiments of evil?

This is a distinction the world simply doesn't get. They believe that if the environment is controlled, the heart will follow meekly along. A government employee once told us that a daycare center in our state was busted from the highest quality rating to the lowest because an inspector discovered "toys of violence" — a handful of two-inch plastic soldiers. O, the horror!

What does this say in a state where one out of twelve employed people are either active duty or civilian workers with the armed services or Coast Guard? A state which includes seven major military bases and a large Coast Guard installation, besides numerous National Guard units? We wonder whether any of the students at that daycare center had parents or relatives serving overseas at the time. Are they being taught that serving their country in that way is somehow shameful? Let's not follow after nonsense like that. The freedom we enjoy was neither won nor kept secure without the carefully controlled application of force.

Principles of Play

This formed the foundation for our practice with our sons. Obviously, we allowed them to have toy weapons, from plastic swords to toy firearms, and we encouraged them to use them correctly. The first need is to distinguish between real and pretend. When Melanie's little brother was young, he found a gun at his grandparents' house and thinking it was a plaything, appeared on the family scene toying with it. Thankfully no harm came of the discovery, but it scared the living daylights out of everyone. Any real firearms in our home are put away and have trigger locks — required by law now, anyway — and toy guns are clearly identified with orange caps on the barrel. What about other people's houses? Best to train our sons how to respect guns (including the concept of *leaving strange guns alone*, like avoiding a strange dog) than depend on other people's safety awareness.

Growing up around guns, we constantly heard the warning to treat every one as if it were loaded. People are often killed by "unloaded" guns, we were told, so you never point a gun anywhere you didn't intend to shoot, even if you "know" the gun is safe. Since their playtime is training for adulthood, we don't allow the boys to point toy guns at each other, either. "Watch where you're pointing that thing," is a frequent reminder at our house, even if "that thing" is a fat finger pointing at a brother.

A larger principle, one that applies to all play, is to stay on the side of the angels. Psalm 14 says *"Fools mock at sin,"* they impudently deride the notion of evil and guilt, and they refuse to consider it a serious matter to violate the law of God. The Bible warns us that children are naturally foolish, so we need to be sure to train them to take God's commandments seriously.[15] The Sermon on the Mount says that if the real act would be sinful, then the imaginary acts we indulge are still sinful; sexual fantasies are spiritual adultery, internalized rage is the spiritual root of murder.[16]

Therefore, we don't allow the boys to pretend to kill anyone real; all their enemies have to be imaginary. This does two things; first, it keeps them away from the sin of rehearsing sin. They don't need practice with that, it seems to come naturally. Secondly, it prevents bad feelings between brothers or friends — no one comes in crying that they were "dead." They have to hunt imaginary bears, not the dog.

We likewise require they play "the good guys." You never see Nazis or desperadoes around here, they're part of the imaginary enemies. We even found a solution to the fascination with pirates — if they want to be swashbuckling, then they have to be privateers.[17] There is a slight problem with swordplay: while pointing a toy gun and shouting "bang" may break the rules, it doesn't actually *injure* anyone. A good whack with a toy sword can raise a real welt, though, so any fencing (a sport, after all) needs some supervision.

While these few rules seem to cut down most of the genuine conflicts in the family, occasionally play will get out of hand anyway. There have been numerous parental armistices over the years, and the garage has been our temporary armory for confiscated weapons. When everyone is over the hurt feeling or general hullabaloo, we'll release them for further military exercises.

Do these considerations apply to other forms of entertainment? You bet. Video games are the prime example, with some very realistic shooting games at the top of the list. Some are hot enough to be simulators for military training, and involve intense first-person situations. These may actually be acceptable for older sons, though much too violent or graphic for younger boys, and not something that anyone should engross themselves in for hours a day. Even the Marines recognize the need to get downtime between missions. Games that invite the player to become a gangster, a car thief, or engage in Mafia-style killings, are beyond the pale—even if the victims are cartoonish.

What about other toys that may be violent in character? We allow a broader range of play when there are no people involved; for example, pretending car crashes and building demolition is focused more on the inanimate objects and the big noise than in murder and mayhem (we would draw the line at attacking little sister's baby dolls with a toy tank). Large scale troop maneuvers with plastic soldiers don't seem troubling even with both sides represented on the field, because the violence is directed against your brother's army, not at him. It can even be a teaching opportunity; one afternoon we found the younger boys mixing the bins, mobilizing Stonewall Jackson and the 101st Airborne against a mixed-arms battalion of astronauts, British grenadiers, and assorted Plains Indians.

As a matter of liberty, we aren't hardlined about every facet of this. We do allow our boys to shoot squirt guns and throw water bombs at each other while playing in the lake. We've found that's more about good-natured getting each other wet and not as much about "killing" each other. Ours aren't engaging in imaginary gun play the same way when it's waterguns - it's like a game of tag to them. We'd judge differently if there was intent to cause trouble between brothers. While we allow all kinds of toy weaponry around the house, we've had to totally ban rubber bands — the time between possession and offense seems to be less than five minutes. Our boys respect guns but can't deal with elastic.

One perceptive mother of a single daughter asked what we thought about action figures. Our boys have never had much interest in the large scale figures like G.I. Joe or the smaller figures associated with movies, comic books, or TV series, though they have collected a few armored knights and such along the way. Based on our standing principles, toys that encourage the imagination toward nobility and honorable service to others are probably acceptable; those which glorify brutality, evil spirituality, or ugliness in general, aren't. One company calls their selection of toys "vision tools," because they're meant to give children a vision for their future lives as men and women in service to God, family, and country. We don't want to give our children tools to establish the wrong kind of vision.

We discuss movies and books elsewhere, but the same principles apply to them as well.

A Time for Real Weapons

It's hard to imagine sometimes, but one day each of our sons will be old enough and mature enough that if he has a need for a real weapon, it will be time to give him that responsibility. Perhaps you hunt, or your friends do, and your son wants to learn how. We know families whose fathers and sons provide most or all of the family's red meat by hunting deer. This is plainly condoned by Scripture; it's also an important part of the ecosystem. In our neighborhood, for example, hunting is not allowed, and the deer walk sedately down the streets and through the yards. It's a beautiful sight, maybe, but kind of tough on the landscaping they eat. In places where natural predators such as wolves have been suppressed, the population of deer and other game animals like rabbits can become environmentally unsupportable. Controlling the population by judicious hunting reduces the threat of starvation and disease on the rest of the herd.

We do teach our sons that even if they are killing a household pest, they should be merciful about it. A skillful hunter kills his prey quickly, without causing a lingering, suffering death. It's one of the reasons we'd recommend learning from experienced sportsmen, in addition to taking the hunter safety courses many areas require before a license is issued. Local chapters of state wildlife authorities and the National Rifle Association offer many alternatives for training and certification.

Once he's successful with this new skill, he'll be proud that he's contributing by providing food for the family and others. Back at home, you will need to work with your son to be sure he keeps weapons and ammunition secured from younger siblings. In our state, it's not just a matter of safety but a legal requirement. There is absolutely no reason a mature son who practices safety can't have guns, bows and arrows, swords or any other reasonable weapon.

It may be that your son has a desire to follow a profession that uses weapons. This frightens many moms. A few years ago someone posted a poem to a local homeschool group talking about a mother's despair with her son joining the military. Many moms wrote in and just *loved* it, but every member who had served in the military (and even their wives) hated it when they saw it. To a man, they said that they didn't want their family feeling sorry for them or worrying themselves sick. They pointed out that God had written the number of their days before there had been one of them and that they were proud to risk their lives to protect our country and what we believe in.

This is a matter of both faith and gender. When men think of war they think of the excitement of combat, of the nobility of laying down their life for a friend, of the principles they would be fighting for. When women think of war, they think of widows, orphans, and bereft parents grieving. It's an entirely different perspective based on who God made us to be. It's not that one perspective is right and the other wrong, but they are different because of our different roles in the world. A mother facing her son going into the military may need to exercise a level of faith to entrust her son to God, an exercise that her son and even her husband may not begin to understand. At that time, it is going to be critical for her to keep womanly fears to herself. Her son is doing a noble and manly thing and he wants her to be proud of him, not sad or scared.

What if the parents have serious, principled misgivings, though? For example, members of some denominations which teach a doctrine of non-resistance may have long-standing theological objections to any kind of armed service. In that case, they should probably consider their son's desire for adventure or his desire to make a tangible difference in the world, and look for an acceptable outlet. He might be directed toward the Coast Guard, fire fighting, emergency medical services, police work, and similar professions which are active and hazardous service that isn't intended for use in warfare. The answer is not to make our sons mild-mannered, but to channel their adventurous desires into places where their family's conscience is not strained — where in fact, they may be doing active acts of mercy.

Conclusion

The Scripture gives plenty of examples of the need for virtuous warriors, for men of arms and integrity, for officers of justice and defense at all levels. With the permission we find in the Bible, we not only allow our sons to play with toy guns and weapons, we encourage it, with proper training in the safe and righteous use of these tools. Pretending to be a soldier in defense of your country, a detective hunting down dangerous counterfeiters, a pioneer tracking bison or mountain lions to feed your family or defend your flock — these are good things. Our sons have hunted invisible bears, fought imaginary invaders, protected General Washington's camp, and repelled boarders with sword and pistol. They have apprehended bootleggers in the Appalachians and served as longbowmen at Poitiers. And no one has drawn blood or shot their eye out.

Taking a reasoned, careful approach to toy weapons as a teaching opportunity allows us to train our sons to respect the real thing. It enhances their view of themselves as men. God made men to be warriors, some with sword, some with the pen, all with the will to resist temptation and strive for righteousness. They will all have to fight evil, sometimes physical, frequently spiritual. Just as we teach them the truth of God's word to better arm them for the spiritual battle, we can help them understand the proper use of physical strength and appropriate weapons in the right causes. Even a cap gun can be wielded for the glory of God.

Notes for Chapter 4

[1] Zechariah 8:4-5

[2] Luke 7:32

[3] Genesis 3:21, 4:1-7, 9:1-4; numerous passages from the institution of Passover in Exodus 12 through Leviticus and Deuteronomy.

[4] Genesis 9:6. The list of offenses to receive the death penalty included murder, rape, and kidnapping, as well as sexual perversion, witchcraft, perjury, and rebellion against parents. See Leviticus 20, Deuteronomy 22, and other places for examples.

[5] Matthew 5:39

[6] Matthew 26:52

[7] John 2:13-17

[8] Luke 3:14

[9] Matthew 8:5-13

[10] Luke 22:36

[11] Philippians 2:25; Philemon 1:2; Ephesians 6:11-17

[12] Romans 13:3-4

[13] 1 Corinthians 6:1-6

[14] Numbers 35:22-28

[15] Proverbs 22:15

[16] Psalm 14:9; Matthew 5:21-28.

[17] Privateers were private ship owners who were given "letters of marque and reprisal", licensing them to pursue and capture vessels of enemy nations in the name of their own country. England, France, and Spain used them against each other for centuries, and during the Revolution, the Continental Congress had more privateers than Navy vessels in service against the British. The Crown considered American privateers as nothing but pirates, only because they considered Congress a den of rebels, not a legitimate national government with sovereignty to issue such letters. The practice died out by the early 20th century, but some members of Congress have suggested reviving the practice against belligerent Middle Eastern regimes.

5

Who's In Charge Here?

The image of a boy and his dog is a cultural icon. We had dogs of many sorts growing up, and wanted our sons to have that experience as well. However, the multiple relocations we underwent between the military and starting a civilian career suggested we wait for a more stable homeplace before getting our sons a dog of their own.

It took a church member's relocation to bring a dog to our lives, and it was a two-year-old black Labrador — a beautiful, well-trained dog, but large and active for children who'd never been around dogs much. We went over to our friends' house to take a look at the dog, but also to gauge the boys' reactions to her.

Well, the boys were fascinated by this sleek, 65-pound animal. The older ones were attracted but a little cautious at this unknown quantity. But our fourth son, Samuel, was fascinating *us*. Though barely five and like his brothers, never having spent time with canines, Samuel marched into the dog's yard and promptly commanded her, "Sit!" Which the dog, being well-trained, promptly did. He then commenced a game of fetch that sealed a friendship in the first five minutes of their meeting — each time, commanding the dog to sit and wait for the throw. It was almost uncanny.

Samuel is the family's Dr. Doolittle. If we visit a friend's farm, the place to look for Samuel is inside the corral, talking in the mule's ear (and the mule politely listening). We've seen him walk outside and pick up song birds, carrying them around like some child St. Francis. He's exceptional that way. However, his first encounter with the dog was emblematic of the relationship of boy and hound. Even though he's just five, he knows he's in charge, and the dog responds.

That's a basic desire of our sons — they want to be in charge. They order the dog around, they boss and bully their younger siblings, they assert authority wherever they can make their voice heard. They're not alone in that, of course; girls can be bossy, too. But God has given men a special role as leaders, and especially as leaders of other men, that requires conscious training and development for our sons' preparation.

What the Bible says about leadership

One of our national ideals is the rugged individualist, the man who rules himself and his domain, and lets nobody dictate what he does or thinks. Ah, freedom! The reality, though, is that man was not created to live alone; first God gave him a wife, then a family, and later a community. Living in proximity to other individualists will eventually lead to conflicts, hot or warm, and a need for judges, rulers, and leaders of one sort or another to guide disputes to a reasonably peaceful conclusion. When the Scripture says that all Israel went to their tents, and *everyone did right in his own eyes*, there was trouble afoot.[1]

There eventually needs to be an authority structure. God ordains jurisdictions of family, church, and state, but each has a leader, and in the first two cases, the role is given to men. That is a matter of some debate in Christian circles, but we take it simply as given in Scripture. In the case of the church, the New Testament speaks of elders and deacons as men.[2] In the family, it says, *Wives, submit to your own husbands, as unto the Lord. For the husband is the head of the wife...*[3]

While the world finds that last teaching offensive, it's partly because the church misses the point sometimes. The whole story is *the husband is the head of the wife, as also Christ is head of the church ... Husbands, love your wives, just as Christ loved the church and gave Himself for her.*[4] Being the head of the household, in God's eyes, means being willing to sacrifice yourself, to *die*, if necessary. That's what Jesus did, and He is held as the example. It's not chauvinism, it's more of chivalry, if you want to call it that.

And if Jesus is the example, what did He do? What did He say to His disciples, whom He was training to lead His church after His return to heaven? Certainly He gave them power over sickness and demons, He gave them the Holy Spirit and promised to guide their words in their moments of stress and need, and assured them of His constant presence and support. But He also told them they must learn to serve: *"If anyone desires to be first, he shall be last of all and servant of all."*[5] Jesus performed the most menial duty of a household servant, washing the feet of His guests, then said to them, *"Do you know what I have done to you? ... I have given you an example, that you should do as I have done to you."*[6] At His last supper before the crucifixion,

> *... there was also a dispute among them, as to which of them should be considered the greatest. And He said to them, "The kings of the Gentiles exercise lordship over them, and those who exercise authority over them are called 'benefactors.' But not so among you; on the contrary, he who is greatest among you, let him be as the younger, and he who governs as he who serves. For who is greater, he who sits at the table, or he who serves? Is*

it not he who sits at the table? Yet I am among you as
the One who serves." [7]

Other versions of this passage say the Gentile rulers "lord it over them." If the Creator and Sustainer of the universe would stoop to wash the feet of His friends, not "lording" over them, then the greatest leader of humanity should be humble like Him, too.

A leader also operates within a command structure. All earthly authority is subordinate to God — the reason we submit to government officials — and there are levels of authority within the state, the church, and the family. Before we give orders, we must be able to take them as well. The Roman centurion in Matthew 8 understood this perfectly; as a military officer, he said, *"I also am a man under authority, having soldiers under me."* No need for the Healer to come to the servant's bedside, the centurion said; just give the order, and I know the power You command will do as you say.[8]

Within that structure, there are both authority and boundaries. Those with authority are expected to be content with their wages and not abuse their position by threats, extortion, and other corruption.[9] In the New Testament, this idea of a bounded authority is applied to military and civilian officials and business leaders, as well as parents. Furthermore, we're told the leader will be judged by a stricter standard than common.[10] No free ride here.

We know manly leadership requires vision, boldness, and action. But the Scripture tells us a godly leader is also a servant, one who understands his place in the chain of command, and one who is content with both the privileges and the limits assigned to him. A leader is held to a high standard. And all this may be harder to achieve than the bold, active, visionary things.

Learn to obey before you learn to lead

Our sons may be destined for greatness, but they aren't born into it. *"Woe to you, O land, when your king is a child,"* says the Preacher in Ecclesiastes. The Lord warns of judgment against Judah and Jerusalem, saying, *"I will give children to be their princes,/And babes shall rule over them."*[11] There are very few leaders in history who simply burst upon the scene, ready to command obedience and respect. In American history, particularly, there is a tradition that a man has to "pay his dues" and work his way up; a commander or supervisor who appears to be inserted over a unit or department with no experience or training is frequently resented and not uncommonly sabotaged by his men. In the War Between the States, both armies were plagued by political generals who wangled themselves appointments by virtue of their position in civil government. A few of them actually did distinguish themselves on the battlefield, but the most successful commanders — and the ones most eagerly followed — were those who did their time as enlisted soldiers and junior officers before taking charge of large units. They learned the business they were in and showed their understanding of obedience to their own authorities before they assumed a higher rank.

Even Jesus demonstrated His understanding of earthly subjection, being an obedient son to Joseph and Mary, revealing His unique nature gradually so that He grew *in favor with God and men.*[12] He not only taught the subordinate relationship of the Son to the Father, He subjected Himself bodily to the will of His Father.[13] A remarkable passage in Hebrews says that *Christ did not glorify Himself to become High Priest ... though He was a Son,* yet *He learned obedience by the things which He suffered.*[14]

Our sons, too, need to learn obedience. When they are accustomed to respect their parents' instructions and wishes, they are better prepared to respect and obey the Lord. That sounds straightforward enough, but anyone who's tried it knows that disciplining boys is frequently exhausting, often frustrating, and seemingly pointless as you deal with the same issues day after day. Yet we can't ignore it; *He who spares his rod hates his son, says the Proverb, But he who loves him disciplines him promptly.*[15] In fact, if we don't provide our sons with the discipline they need, the Bible says it is as much as disowning them.[16] The Puritan Thomas Brooks said, "God had one Son without corruption, but no son without correction" — seeing that even the sinless Christ suffered punishment for His people.[17]

One of the difficult dynamics is the tension between the young male and the mother who has authority over him. It's an old problem; the French essayist Michel de Montaigne, advising a noblewoman on the raising of her son, wrote nearly five centuries ago,

> ... 'tis the general opinion of all, that a child should not be brought up in his mother's lap. Mothers are too tender, and their natural affection is apt to make the most discreet of them all so overfond, that they [cannot] find in their hearts to give them due correction for the faults they commit ... And yet there is no remedy; whoever will breed a boy to be good for anything when he comes to be a man, must be no means spare him when he is young...[18]

God made boys — all of them — to be leaders. Nearly every boy will one day lead a household, and in likelihood will have some role of leadership elsewhere, whether at church, on the job, or over a club, team, or community activity. They have an instinct to take charge, and that desire to rule and command needs training. Unfortunately, it will often combine with the sin nature to become a real challenge to his parents, especially his mother.

Our sons know that Dad is the head of the household. However, it's usually Mom who is close by during the day, and therefore executing the majority of the discipline. We find that the threat "Wait 'til your father gets home!" is not very effective, preferring a friend's succinct rule, "Penalty is taken at the point of infraction." However, we also find it necessary — and helpful — to carefully explain the full chain of command to the boys: God is in charge of everything, and He gives Dad authority over the family; Dad is in charge of everything in the family, and delegates authority to Mom; Mom has authority over the children; the boys have authority over themselves, the dog and the fish.

So we make it clear to our sons that Mom's directions are backed up by Dad's authority, and if they disobey Mom, they're really disputing with Dad. Sometimes Dad has to get toe-to-toe with a young buck and explain, man-to-man, that he has now crossed the line and upset Dad's bride, and Dad won't stand for it. There's no question about the children playing the two parents against each other, because Dad *always* backs up Mom, and Mom *always* defers to Dad.

In a way, it helps a young man's pride to understand that when his mother is giving direction to a 16-year-old who's taller than her, she stands as the agent of Dad's authority (or of God the Father's, if she is a single mother); he's not a three-year-old taking direction from Mommy. It's easier for the young man to submit to a woman when he realizes the whole chain of command. Likewise, it helps them obeying parents generally when a young man comprehends that his parents are acting as *God's* agents, the local authorities which He appointed on his behalf. When you honor your parents, you're obeying God.

A matter of discipline

And when they don't? Then it's time to administer corrective action. Some people — not all of them parents, by any
means — are opposed to any sort of discipline, even non-physical punishments like "time-out"; they call it "coercive parenting." What they actually do is elevate the child's autonomy to the
level of those who are responsible to God for him, harming both
the parent and the child.

Others discipline harshly, in anger. Sometimes it is a person
who had intended to not correct a child at all, but lost their temper
after a prolonged challenge. This leads to self-recrimination ("See
how *evil* I am! Exactly why I should *never* punish a child!"). In the
hands of a cunning child, it opens up a broad path for manipula-
tive handling. We've known both types.

The word of God gives us the balance. We are told to use physical punishment and not to withhold correction, but we are also
warned not to provoke our children to wrath, which can happen
if they perceive our correction to be unjust or personal.[19] Often
parents fail in both respects.

Many people, and often mothers (as Montaigne suggested),
believe that they are being loving and merciful by using "time out"
and other non-physical corrections instead of imposing physical
discipline on their boys. Besides the fact that it doesn't seem to
impress boys much, this approach goes against the Biblical pattern. "Discipline" comes from the same root as "disciple," and
it carries the connotation of teaching and restraining the self
against temptation, whether the temptation to commit known
sin, or the temptation to omit a positive duty. In response to sin,
discipline is meant to bring about repentance and restoration.

In fact, the idea that a parent should be a disciplinarian is one way God chose to describe Himself. *For whom the Lord loves He corrects,* says the Proverb, *Just as a father the son in whom he delights.*[20] Do we love our children more than God loves His? Well, He tells us that He is in the business of dealing out correction to them. Even more strongly, the New Testament repeats the precept, and emphasizes it — *For whom the Lord loves He chastens,/And scourges every son whom He receives.*[21] And rather than nurturing ill feelings between us, *Behold,* it says, *happy is the man whom God corrects;/Therefore do not despise the chastening of the Almighty.*[22] We are blessed when God takes us to the woodshed. The Bible says so.

It says not to despise discipline, but it doesn't say we have to like it. *Now no chastening seems to be joyful for the present, but painful; nevertheless, afterward it yields the peaceable fruit of righteousness to those who have been trained by it.*[23] This is in the context of God's correction of His children, and it is part of the pattern of our correction of our own — it is an expression of our love, it is temporarily unpleasant, but should lead to teaching, repentance, and restoration.

Thanks to some good counsel and advice from Lou Priolo's book, *The Heart of Anger,* we developed a pattern for discipline when our children are in sin.[24] First, we make sure we are able to approach the situation calmly and judiciously; we may need to take a few minutes to pray and quiet ourselves, to avoid dealing out punishment in anger. It may be helpful to give the child a few minutes to calm down as well, to step away from the conflict and consider. When we have control of ourselves, we administer the type and amount of discipline which is just and in accordance with Scripture.

At that point the teaching comes in. We'll ask the son, "Were you wrong? What did you do wrong?" The point is to make the child face his sin; when God asked Adam and Eve, *"Where are you? ... What* is *this you have done?*", He wasn't looking for information; He was forcing them to confront their fall from innocence. It's much harder for the child to deal with the attitude of his heart than the discomfort of a spanking, which is why we press the questions on him. A child who has trouble admitting his wrong is not repentant. (If you have trouble enforcing this, it may be that you are confronting mere annoyance as if it were sin, and disciplining the wrong way for the wrong behavior. More on that later.)

The next question is, "What should you have done?" This can be a teaching moment for parents, too, because it will sometimes uncover things we've left untaught. It is eye-opening when you learn your child truly didn't know how to handle a situation; a swift punch or a cruel word may have seemed the natural response to their frustration of the moment. Use the opportunity to instruct them—the preferred response may have been, "Go get a parent;" "Share with my brother;" or "Leave the situation;" but your child should finish this disciplinary session with a clear alternative for next time.

We insist that they ask for forgiveness and seek it from whomever they've wronged. Require Biblical language—"Please forgive me" seeks to restore a relationship, while "I'm sorry" may secretly mean anything from "I'm sorry I got caught" to "I feel wretched." The restoration of fellowship is the picture of God's forgiveness that we want to teach our children.

That means, of course, that we have to model God's forgiveness. When we forgive them, we tell them so, we pray with them, and we go forward in peace. They will need a clear expression of the parents' love, even if they're "tough." We noticed several years ago that our boys would almost always go away and get a minor "owie" after they had been disciplined—a stubbed toe, a stumble and fall, a paper cut. It was always minor, but they would make a big deal about it. They needed someone to "love on them" a bit, even the older boys; they may be too big for a lap, but never too big for a manly hug and a slap on the back.

Older sons may need reassurance that they can forgive themselves. Some may hang on to a lingering guilt as if continuing self-flagellation will somehow balance the moral universe, refusing to accept the offered forgiveness. This is not only exasperating to live around, it's unbiblical; when God forgives, it is completely over. We could never work our way into a state of undeserved grace, and we can never add anything to our restoration by our own acts of contrition.

Once your son has asked for forgiveness and received it, the case is closed. It would be unjust to bring it back to light. The Psalmist says that *As far as the east is from the west,/So far has He removed our transgressions from us,* and God Himself says, *"I, even I, am He who blots out your transgressions for My own sake; and I will not remember your sins."* [25] Can we do less? Paul warns us that true love *thinks no evil,* or as some translations render it, *does not take into account a wrong suffered.* [26] Love does not keep an account book of grievances, to be brought out at opportune moments to properly humble someone. Fellowship is restored, without reservation.

This is the difficulty with "time out" punishments that focus on exclusion from the fellowship of the family. Exclusionary punishments send the child away from the love and wisdom of his parents to brood in the corner, feeling angry and sorry for themselves in the lack of discipline and teaching. The fear of abandonment and rejection is deep in a small child. How much better to correct the sin and heal the broken fellowship quickly!

Yelling and verbal abuse is similarly non-productive. When the spanking is over, we seldom remember the discomfort; God has given us a remarkably unhelpful memory when it comes to pain. Harmful words, though, can be replayed endlessly in our minds and continue to hurt years later. We should be *speaking the truth in love* to our children, especially when it involves rebuke or correction.[27]

One turning point in our understanding of Biblical discipline was early in our marriage, when we watched a video series taught by Dr. James Dobson. He made a particular point of distinguishing between rebellion and childish irresponsibility. The Bible makes a clear distinction — foolishness is the normal behavior of children, while rebellion is a sin like necromancy.[28] Rebellious behavior, such as deliberate disobedience or defiance, should receive prompt, firm discipline and correction. Remember the chain of command — seeking to overthrow the parents' authority is an attack on God's authority which He delegated to them. We owe it to *God* to take action against insurrection.

On the other hand, the boy who runs inside to show off a new-captured toad, tracking mud on the floor and letting in the flies through the open door, has certainly been careless and probably discourteous to Mom, but it's not an intentional sin. The five-year-old boy who makes lunch without permission, bringing Daddy *five* bologna sandwiches because he thought Dad would like all he could get, is just being overenthusiastic, not subversive. The teenager who fixes his bicycle and rides off, leaving the tools on the steps, is being thoughtless, not conspiratorial.

To be honest, sometimes these incidents should cause us to reflect on our training as parents — perhaps we should have given them more supervision, for example. Still, we need to train them to prevent these kinds of lapses as well. This is a great opportunity "to let the punishment fit the crime," as Gilbert & Sullivan's Mikado said. Impose some real-world consequences, like cleaning the carpet or killing the flies. Irresponsibility like losing or damaging a school book — yes, even homeschoolers lose school books — results in a child buying the replacement with his birthday money.[29] Such corrective action is measured, limited, and appropriate for the offense; even the offender should be able to see that.

Treating this kind of childishness as though it were a blatant and intentional attack on the entire God-given family structure, though — in other words, treating our annoyance as if causing it was a sin — can outrage our children's sense of justice, and as adolescence approaches, it can feed the "No one understands me!" attitude so tempting to young men.

Speaking of adolescence, we found it brought an incredible excess of testosterone into the house. Some days it seems everyone with a Y-chromosome and at least twelve candles on his birthday cake is just spoiling for a fight. Sometimes, though, it's hard to pinpoint just what sin needs correction. We take the army approach, "Drop and give me ten." The boys do push-ups, run the stairs, do crunches. It has the benefit of not only punishing belligerence, but also providing an outlet for some of that aggression. It's a guy thing, too; it doesn't make them feel childish. Unfortunately, it's not unusual to find several young men doing push-ups at the same time. Still, it works; it makes them stronger, too.

Developing the next generation's leaders

It may seem that much of the discipling process is a negative action, to stop misbehaviors. If that's all it is, we're missing the duty to protect, develop, and strengthen the confidence and leadership skills of our sons. We need to consciously seek opportunities to stretch and train them for future service.

One thing we have seen, time and time again, is that opportunities for leadership are often bestowed on people who are not the most brilliant or celebrated, but are available and willing. A while back, at a meeting of a student group we attended, the high schoolers were discussing the coming year's plans. Most of the boys were studiously cool and indifferent; only one young man was willing to step forward and assume responsibility. He became the group's leader by default. Similar things have happened to each of us as adults; it behooves us then to give our sons the foundation that allows them to seize the opportunity to serve the Lord and the community without paralyzing fear or cultivated apathy.

There is a difference between qualification and opportunity. Qualification is a matter of character and experience, some of which we can train for, some which we encourage, some which come about Providentially. For opportunity, though, we can work consciously to remove barriers which block our sons' path.

The ability to speak comfortably to groups of people is a major help. A willingness to face a crowd sets a young man apart; public speaking is said to be more frightening than everything but snakes to the average person, and even death runs behind the fear of a microphone.

This begins early in life; a boy who is subjected to scorn and public criticism, even in his own family, often begins constructing a protective shell. He may hide his shyness under a façade of "cool," a withering irony of his own, or a wall of silence, whether fearful or arrogant. We try to make a point of correcting our sons in private, where possible, and focusing criticism on behaviors rather than his self-worth. "You are acting like a fool," as strong and harsh as that is, has a different impact than, "You *are* a fool"—the first offers hope, an expectation even, that the boy is capable of higher things. The latter doesn't, and a boy who is routinely cut down in his own family may not want to risk it from his friends or the public in general.

There is an element, too, of selfishness underlying shyness. Melanie is widely known as an outgoing, engaging speaker who interacts with all kinds of people in small groups and large. She is also extremely shy, a suggestion which most of her friends would laugh at. She can talk easily and eloquently to an audience of 500 strangers, but has to work herself up to making a phone call.

What she realized is that shyness elevates our own comfort over courtesy, obedience to parents, or even faithfulness to God; it is considering our own needs ("wants," really) above others. If an adult asks a question to a child and the child's response is to bury his face in Mama's skirt and refuse to answer, it can be an awkward moment for the adult. Similarly, the person an older child feels too embarrassed to speak to may feel left out or snubbed. A desire to avoid comments or criticism may prevent us from speaking up for truth, sharing our faith, or defending an embattled colleague. It effectively neutralizes our outreach to a world that desperately needs it.

Furthermore, shyness interfered with what Melanie wanted to accomplish in life, so she decided to overcome it. The best way to get over public discomfort is to confront it head on, a little bit at a time. Melanie makes a point to be outgoing, even when she feels shy inside. When she's in a group, she looks for the person who seems uncertain or embarrassed, and goes to be a friend to them and draw them into the fellowship. Young men can try the same approach.

We look for opportunities for the boys to master this fear. We start by asking our sons to take turns reading aloud in our family devotions and reading times. Even new readers can soldier through one verse, if a parent or older sibling prompts them for the difficult words, and every man should be ready to read the Bible to his family and pray out loud briefly when asked.

When we go on field trips, we tell the boys to come up with one question each to ask the guides; this allows the boys to think ahead about what they're going to see, and at the same time prepare a short public statement. It also encourages the museum staff when they see young people engaging the exhibit; we've been given the impromptu deluxe tour more than once because the children show an interest. Museum staff routinely tell us how much it means to them when students ask thoughtful questions and show appreciation for their presentation; the average school group too frequently does not.

Public speaking contests, such as those sponsored by 4-H, give a structured opportunity even to young students. Older students can take part in debate and speaking contests sponsored by the American Legion, chamber of commerce, or other organizations. Sometimes the prizes are there for the taking. Recently three of our sons took part in giving presentations at a county-wide event; the organizers were only able to find six participants, and three of them were from our family!

The more your boys speak in public, the more comfortable they will become doing so. It's an invaluable skill for ministry, public service, and career.

Starting Small

We can give our sons opportunities to show leadership even within the family. When they reach eleven, each of our boys attends a babysitting course taught at the local hospital. There is no intention that they would ever "sit" for someone outside the family, but it is meant to give them more skills to watch over their younger siblings. If both parents need to leave the house, we will specifically designate the brother in charge and deputize them with a measure of authority. The announcement is something like, "While we are gone, John will be in charge. If you give him a difficult time, you are violating *our* authority. If you disobey him, you are disobeying *us,* and you will have to answer for it when we return."

It's not always the oldest brother, either. Recently the senior brother at home was engulfed in preparation for Advanced Placement exams. With his knowledge and agreement, we designated the next older brother to watch over the younger ones so the eldest could study.

The brother in charge is given to understand the limits to that authority — the greatest punishment he can levy is to send an offender to bed early; the deputizing is temporary and expires when the parents return; and he is reminded he has not been crowned "tyrant," We find that the system works pretty well — with some coaching over the phone, from time to time.

Servant Leaders

Our sons need to understand the full picture of leadership, too. Many people will agree to a leadership role only because they see a personal benefit or an opportunity for public acclaim. We frequently meet parents who will lead an activity for their child's benefit but not to help others, or who agree to serve as a "vice-something or other" but are suddenly unavailable if they are needed to step up to the lead role.

The reality of leadership is just as Christ said — service. The faithful leader knows the responsibility means demands on time and attention, dealing with unpleasant situations and people, working through conflicts of personnel or resources, and facing the downside of "glory" — always living under the magnifying glass. It is often lonely; the point man is the one who draws fire, and he often doesn't see the followers behind him — he's in front of them, right? We want our sons to be prepared both to stand in the spotlight, and to stand in the gaps. We serve because there is a need, and if there are rewards as well, that's a side benefit. Our ultimate reward isn't here on earth. Our sons need to understand this and embrace it.

Conclusion

Our sons will not always be in charge, but all of them will be in charge at some time in their lives. They will not remain children, but they will always be in subjection to authority somewhere in their daily lives. When the need arises, they should be ready and equipped to speak up, to step forward, to carry the burden of leadership without creating a dictatorship of "me." The idea of leading by serving, the example of Christ, is a difficult one to follow, but it needs to be taught and lived out in the lives of parents as well as sons. The world needs them, the church needs them, and their families — even if only themselves alone — need them to be godly leaders.

NOTES FOR CHAPTER 5

[1] 1 Kings 12:16; Judges 17:6

[2] 1 Timothy 3:2 ("bishop" or overseer being synonymous with elders or presbyters, see Titus 1:5-6); 1 Timothy 3:12

[3] Ephesians 5:22-24

[4] Ephesians 5:24-25

[5] Mark 9:35

[6] John 13:12-16

[7] Luke 22:24-27

[8] Matthew 8:5-13

[9] The tax collectors and soldiers who met John the Baptist, Luke 3:12-14; Zacchaeus the tax collector, Luke 19:1-10.

[10] James 3:1

[11] Ecclesiastes 10:16; Isaiah 3:4

[12] Luke 2:51-53

[13] Matthew 26:36-44

[14] Hebrews 5:5-8

[15] Proverbs 13:24

[16] Hebrews 12:8

[17] Thomas Brooks (1608-1680), *Precious Remedies Against Satan's Devices* (Carlisle, PA: Banner of Truth, 1990), p. 86.

[18] Michel de Montaigne (1533-1592), "On the education of children", *Essays*, I:25. Translated by Charles Cotton in *Great Books of the Western World*, vol. 25 (Chicago: Encyclopedia Britannica, 1952), p. 66.

[19] Proverbs 22:15; Proverbs 23:13; Ephesians 6:4

[20] Proverbs 3:12

[21] Hebrews 12:6

[22] Job 5:17

[23] Hebrews 12:11

[24] Lou Priolo, *The Heart of Anger* (Amityville, NY: Calvary Press, 1997)

[25] Psalm 103:12; Isaiah 43:25

[26] 1 Corinthians 13:5 (NASB)

[27] Ephesians 4:15

[28] Proverbs 22:15; Deuteronomy 21:18-21

[29] There are several books which suggest Biblical passages relating to specific misbehaviors. One of our favorites is Pam Forster's *For Instruction in Righteousness* (www.Doorposts.com). It's a fantastic resource for Biblical consequences for particular sins as well as foolishness and immature behavior. We use it whenever we find ourselves complaining, "The children are always ... " — a sure sign more instruction is needed. The children groan when we bring it out, but almost invariably, reading and discussing the passages will be blessed by the Spirit, and repentence and forgiveness between all of us is the result.

6

Racing to Win

When we lived in Louisiana, we had good family friends who moved from their home near Baton Rouge to Jackson, Mississippi, a good two hours away. Not long after, we were traveling back to visit our family in the Carolinas and made the slight detour to see them again. We pulled up in their driveway; the door of our station wagon opened and our oldest son, about five years old at the time, jumped out. His friend emerged from the house about the same time. They met in the front yard and the conversation went something like this:

> *"Hi, John!"*
> *"Hi, Peter!"*
> *"Aarrgh!"*
> *"Rrrrr!"*

And they locked arms and rolled in the grass, trying to pin one another to the ground. Both mothers, stunned, circled around them saying, "Boys! Boys!" The fathers, on the other hand, ignored this behavior as perfectly normal.

Mothers are made to nurture. They want everyone to be happy. They want everyone to win. They try to rewrite the rules of our board games so no one loses, and delight to find toys that feature "cooperative play." It extends into the schoolroom, too; the idea of cooperative learning where students work together in groups and everyone shares the same work and same grade was definitely invented by women.

Boys just don't think that way. They love to try their strength, whether physical, intellectual, or emotional, against others. They want to see where they stack up. They love to compete; they love to win; and sometimes they would rather lose than not try. Maybe some boys seem to avoid competitions, but they probably just haven't had a chance to compete on their strengths. It's deep seated in the male psyche. It is normal male behavior to say "Hello" and proceed to test your mettle against the other guy. Nothing to see here, folks, just move along.

Future leaders

Our Father made our boys to grow up to be leaders. They will lead in the world and lead in the church. Even those who aren't called to lead the church and never have the opportunity to lead the community, those who seem destined to be subordinates, will still lead their families. The quietest, shyest boy will one day be the head of his household. This may be why boys love competition so — it gives them a chance to see if they are worthy to be the leader in that area.

Melanie majored in biology in college. She remembers studying about the pecking order — the idea that in groups of some kinds of animals, a hierarchy will develop: the toughest chicken rules the roost and pecks on anyone he pleases, the next toughest chicken can peck anyone but the top chicken, and on down to the scrawny little bird that everyone else pecks on. Picking on anyone who isn't tougher than you is hardly a righteous act, but Melanie often thinks about this when she watches groups of boys. The nicest, kindest boy, who would never think of being ugly to those weaker than he is, still wants to know where he is in the "pecking order." He wants to know who is strongest, who is smartest, who can bend his thumb backwards the farthest, who can burp the loudest ... you get the picture. He may never want to use that information to "peck on" anyone, but he wants to test his strengths against others.

Like anything, this desire can take a righteous direction or turn into sin. We've seen the unrighteous kind in our home all too often. Some days there seems to be a pestering competition going on. The older bullies the younger, the younger provokes the older, the one in the middle goads them both on for sheer entertainment. It's a race to the bottom, a competition to see who can be the biggest pest.

Proverbs 6:16-19 says that

> *These six things the LORD hates,*
> *Yes, seven are an abomination to Him:*
> *A proud look,*
> *A lying tongue,*
> *Hands that shed innocent blood,*
> *A heart that devises wicked plans,*
> *Feet that are swift in running to evil,*
> *A false witness who speaks lies,*
> *And one who sows discord among brethren.*

It was a shock to our whole family to realize that the Lord rates "sowing discord among brethren" with lying and shedding innocent blood. It's an important concept to teach your sons.

Another unrighteous result of this desire is bragging — using our strengths to glorify ourselves rather than the Creator who gave them to us. Paul says in Galatians 6:14, "*But God forbid that I should boast, except in the cross of our Lord Jesus Christ,*" and the cross is certainly not what our boys are bragging about. The Lord

Himself told Jeremiah, *"Let not the wise man glory in his wisdom,/ Let not the mighty man glory in his might,/Nor let the rich man glory in his riches;/But let him who glories glory in this,/That he understands and knows Me ... "* [1]

Again, boasting is behavior that needs to be corrected and taught against, especially when the bragging becomes physically or emotionally abusive, when it turns into bullying. As believers we should be showing meekness and mercy, not taking advantage of the weaknesses of others.

The biblical view of competition

Is competition all wrong? We picked up a tract at a book fair once that argued that it was. What does the Word say? It appears to give the opposite teaching; God uses the image of competition repeatedly as an example for us to follow or an illustration of spiritual truth. In the Christian life, we are encouraged to *"run with endurance the race that is set before us."* [2] In the life of the church, we are told to *"outdo one another in showing honor."* [3] The fact that some win and some don't should not put us off; God says to use that knowledge as a spur to try harder. *"Do you not know that those who run in a race all run, but one receives the prize? Run in such a way that you may obtain it."* [4]

This is balanced by God's reminder of two factors — the need for discipline and obedience, and our dependence on Him in all things. Paul wrote to Timothy, *"If anyone competes in athletics, he is not crowned unless he competes according to the rules."* [5] To the Romans he said to keep in mind that *"it is not of him who wills, nor of him who runs, but of God who shows mercy."* [6]

What to make of this? Simply that competition, properly framed and understood, is a healthy and even biblical part of life. The

Lord would not encourage us to use an ungodly pursuit as an example and role model, and He points to the challenge of competition over and over as a metaphor for the Christian life. He even encourages us to strive to win.

The Puritan view of games and competition

A college friend of Hal's once challenged him on his knowledge of the Puritans, asking if he was aware of their teaching on games. Hal knew better than to form his whole conception on *The Scarlet Letter*, probably the limit of what most Americans think they know, but he had to admit the question stumped him. Weren't the Puritans too serious for amusements? The answer was yes, Puritans were serious, but they found a biblical rationale for entertainment and recreation, too. William Perkins wrote, in typically systematic fashion, that:

> *Games may be divided into three sorts: games of wit or industry, games of hazard, and a mixture of both. Games of wit or industry are such as are ordered by the skill and industry of man. Of this sort are shooting in the longbow, shooting in the caliver [an early form of matchlock gun], running, wrestling, fencing, music, and the games of chess and draughts [which we call checkers] ... These, and all of this kind, wherein the industry of the mind and body hath the chiefest stroke, are* **very commendable, and not to be disliked.**[7]

So much for the kill-joy image of the Puritans. Young man, he says, rejoice in profitable, Christ-honoring competition — shoot, spar, and castle kingside for the glory of God!

Making competition a good part of our sons' lives

S o, how can competition and the desire to compete be a good thing in our sons' lives?

For one thing, competition can be a tremendous motivating force for improvement. Our local homeschool support group does a Geography Bee that qualifies winners to compete at the state level of the National Geographic Bee. The first year, no one was particularly excited about it in advance, but then our oldest son came in second in our group. The next year he was determined to win. He did and passed the qualifying test for the state competition. Once there, he made it all the way to fourth place in the state. Well, the Youngs were hooked. Not only did John become passionate about learning geography, but all his brothers did, too. We have maps of the states and the world under plastic on our kitchen table (typical comment: "No, Hunan Province is located over there under the green beans.") and lots of atlases, globes, and more maps around the house. John eventually made it to number two in the state, and everyone after John has worked hard to compete in this area; his next two brothers have made it to the state competition as well. Folks often ask what we use to teach geography — even public school teachers, impressed by the homeschoolers' performance at the state competition - but we have to admit we don't, really. There's no need. The fun of competition has encouraged the boys to seek out and study geography far more than anything we could "teach" them. Our fourth son reads geography textbooks now because, as he said, he doesn't want to let the family down, despite our strong reassurances that we have no such expectation of him. The desire to compete, the hope to win has motivated them tremendously.

The same thing happened to us just last year. Our third son Matthew is the sports fan of the family, and last spring he talked his brothers into going out for contact football with a local homeschool league in the fall. They had to come up with a huge amount of money — nearly $900 for the four of them — to buy their equipment for the first year, and between saving all their birthday gifts and grabbing every bit of paying yard work and house cleaning they could, they managed to earn it all for themselves!

Once they began to play and were praised for their toughness, they were hooked. Boys who had tended to absorb themselves in books and computers on the couch suddenly burst into activity: exercising, watching what they ate, practicing and challenging one another in the yard. The competition did something for them which we were never able to impose on them effectively.

Academic incentive, too

You can use competition to motivate your boys in academics, too. Math has always been a trial for us at that 9-12 age range, especially. It seems like the boys could take hours to complete just one lesson. Some moms we know decided there were too many problems, so they just told their children to do all the odd or even problems. Melanie has a problem with this because math is an exercise that gets easier the more you do; it becomes automatic. One solution we found was to have the children compete against themselves. If they beat a personal best time in doing one lesson or on one fact sheet, they get a treat. Now our treats were never all that exciting — perhaps a couple of gummy bears or something more healthy. It was really just the competition and the fact there was a prize. It was amazing how much more quickly lessons would get done.

The boys invented a variation on this themselves. Even though all our children are in different levels of math, they found it really took about the same amount of time to do a lesson whether you were in the fourth grade or seventh grade book,[8] so they would compete to see who could finish their math lessons the fastest. You may be wondering if they would just race through and do the lesson poorly. Melanie said she never noticed much decrease in accuracy, if any, but there was a *drastic* decrease in doodling and staring out the window![9]

Another type of competition is playing games within the family. For years our oldest children wanted to play board games, but it was hard because none of the little ones were able to hold their own in a game yet. We had to find a way to play as a family before everyone left home. We decided to have each of the older children or adults take a little partner. The little ones were delighted! All they really wanted to do was to throw the dice and move the "man," so with an older child to plan strategy and a little one to make the moves, the older children were able to compete all out. This made everyone happy. It also built happy memories between the brothers, and we soon began to see older children and younger children developing special relationships and wanting to be partners. This was a blessing to us.

We have a favorite all-family competition that we love to do at Hal's mom's lake camp. We all gather in the front room, sitting on chairs and piled all over the floor. We play charades with unusual topics: historical figures, songs and hymns, and movies (we are all into Christian filmmaking, so we're film buffs). The one or two actors (this is a great place for little/big partnerships as well) stand up in the doorway of the eating area, which is raised a step. They tell us their category and act it out while we all guess. We have had a blast doing this. It is something everyone enjoys and the laurels do not always go to the oldest, either.

Lessons to teach and learn in competition

There are so many things to teach our sons in competition: remember Paul's admonition to play by the rules. We need to teach them good sportsmanship, to show love to one another even in victory or defeat. Our friend Earl Pendleton organized a football league for homeschoolers, now serving over seven hundred young athletes a year and even drawing players from out of state. One distinctive of his league is the emphasis on sportsmanship — winning teams don't gloat, losing teams don't sulk, and players never talk back to referees. When a player is hurt, both teams kneel where they are on the field and pray until the player is helped to the bench. One of the referees, a professional hired by the league, told one of our sons that he and his fellow officials loved to work the homeschool games because the attitudes were so much better than the other leagues they worked. Our sons can show a Christian testimony while competing as hard as they can.

Fortitude and endurance in reaching a goal is a good lesson of competition. You have to study spelling for many hours to prepare to compete in a bee or run for many miles to prepare to win a race. The preparation is often boring or painful or time-consuming, though it is often the most valuable part of the process in how your life is impacted by what you learn, whether skills or knowledge or fitness. The thrill of competition can help our sons make it through this difficult personal development.

We can also teach them about teamwork. Teamwork needs patience with the weaknesses of others. Having younger partners really helps this one. Teamwork means a willingness to sacrifice your own desires for the betterment of the group. One of my sons dreamed of being a quarterback, but that is not where his team needed him — they need his bulk and strength on the line (even though a coach remarked, "Some of these linemen have a really good arm.") He has to learn to get over the disappointment and do what's best for the team. That's a great preparation for adulthood. How many times do we as adults want something just for ourselves, just some "me time," but know that it isn't the best thing for the family? Getting up in the middle of the night to care for a baby or comfort a sick or frightened child, or even a father's getting up to leave for work before dawn, requires a willingness to lay down your own desires for the good of the family. Sons can begin to learn this in team play.

Families should be cautious about too much, too

Families, especially big ones, need to be cautious on the other side of this issue as well, though. There is such a thing as destructive competition, or maybe good competition that has a negative impact on the side. What is the balance? One season we decided our sons would play community baseball. At that time, we only had three sons old enough to play, but it nearly killed us. Their ages were just far enough apart that they played in three separate leagues; often practice and games were scheduled at conflicting times. We didn't have a meal together for weeks and were constantly separated, trying to make sure someone was at everyone's practice and game.

We couldn't keep that up past the first year, but we know families that pursue that kind of schedule from baseball to soccer to football to basketball — year round, and round and round. How do they maintain any family life outside the field and the bleachers?

One solution we found was to seek out homeschool leagues wherever possible. They often are more family-friendly, scheduling practices at the same time and location where possible, and grouping games to allow families with multiple ages to participate. Where there are no homeschool leagues, it may be a ministry of sorts to organize one, or to seek out and recruit someone who can.

Another solution might be to limit your family to one ball season a year. What is doable for an eight-week sprint may wreck your family life if extended to back-to-back seasons.

What if there is no suitable league in your area, and no possibility of starting one? There are other competitive sports that only require two players, like tennis or racquetball, or can even be done solo like golf, cycling, or running, competing against the stopwatch or scorecard. Even things like canoeing, fishing, or hunting can be turned into a challenge to meet and surpass. Theodore Roosevelt was fond of taking visitors on straight-line walks, picking a distant landmark and committing to a beeline path — over, under, and through all obstacles, whether fences, creeks, rocks or farm buildings. The important thing is that your boys have an outlet to compete in, even against themselves, and a chance to use their bodies and get out and move. This really helps with too much testosterone in the house, too!

What if your son is "gifted"?

We have served on the board of our state homeschool association for many years, and there is an ongoing debate about whether homeschoolers should agitate for access to public school athletic programs. Our organization actually began organizing state conferences and championships to provide an outlet for families who were convinced their ninth grader was the next Michael Jordan or Kobe Bryant and were thinking of ditching home education to be sure their student didn't miss out on high school locker room culture. Well, maybe that wasn't foremost in their thoughts, but it was straight ahead in their course of direction.

We parents have got to be the adults in this picture. Hal inter-
viewed a high-ranking officer of our state's high school athletic
association, who said that parents who were so optimistic often
did not have a proper perspective about their child's talents. "The
statistics say that less than one half of one percent of our students
will go on to play at college at any level," he said. This association,
by the way, oversees 150,000 high school athletes in a state that
includes perennial athletic powerhouses like Duke University
and the University of North Carolina. "The purpose" of high
school athletics, he continued, "is not, and never has been, to
prepare students to go on. It's an anomaly, and wonderful, if you
do, but it's just a nice by-product. This is meant to build better
citizens ... [and] provide a great learning laboratory to dedica-
tion and teamwork."[10]

In other words, if those statistics are accurate, there is only a
1 in 200 chance that a given student, boy or girl, who made the
team in high school will ever have the opportunity to play ball
in any sport, at any level of college; the chances for the professional level are smaller still. Even if that truly is possible, isn't it
more important that they were grounded in the Word of God and
discipled by their fathers? That can't happen if they are so busy
that they never really get to talk with their dads. Dads watching
at practice is a good thing, but if that is all that happens between
father and son, both of them have lost something valuable.

Conclusion

Competition is loved by boys and is often good for them. The
Bible uses athletic competition as an analogy for the Christian life,
with rules to obey, a struggle to overcome, and even a desire to
come out on top of the field. It's not a bad thing at all, if kept in
the proper perspective. A healthy spirit of competition can spur
our sons to greater achievement, can build cameraderie in the

family and between friends, and can encourage them to step out for opportunities in business and ministry. It makes doing hard things more palatable and can teach some important life lessons as well. It's got to be directed in a godly way, though, and it has to be kept in proportion for our families. That's our job to manage.

NOTES FOR CHAPTER 6

[1] Jeremiah 9:23-24

[2] Hebrews 12:1

[3] Romans 12:10 (ESV)

[4] 1 Corinthians 9:24

[5] 2 Timothy 2:5

[6] Romans 9:16

[7] See "Recreation", in I.D.E. Thomas, compiler, *The Golden Treasury of Puritan Quotations* (Carlisle, PA: Banner of Truth Trust, 1989), pp. 232-233. Perkins goes on to distinguish between games of pure chance, of which he disapproves, and games which use dice or other tools of chance to represent the unknown factors of war or Providence, leaving the outcome of the game to skill. He offered four guidelines for making the best use of our recreational opportunities:

> Rule 1. We are to make choice of recreations that are of least offense and best report.
>
> Rule 2. Our recreations must be profitable to ourselves and others, and they must also tend to the glory of God.
>
> Rule 3. The end of our recreation must be to refresh our bodies and minds.
>
> Rule 4. Recreation must be moderate and sparing, even as the use of meat and drink and rest.

[8] For what it's worth, we've used Saxon Math through algebra.

[9] This can work with adult males, too. Karl Rove, the chief of staff for President George W. Bush, wrote in the *Wall Street Journal* that for years, he and the President raced each other to see who could read the most books in a year. Rove started it as a new year's resolution and the President turned it into a contest. Rove said he always won, the President claiming he was busy leading the free world, but that Bush found the competition kept him focused; busy or not, Bush—who was a history major at Yale - typically finished a book a week while in office ("Bush is a book lover", *WSJ*, 12/26/08).

[10] Interview with Rick Strunk, associate executive director of the N.C. High School Athletic Association. His remarks were included in a story in the May 2009 issue of *Carolina Journal*, a publication of the John Locke Foundation in Raleigh, N.C.

7

DOING REAL THINGS

When you have a large family, you learn something quickly — every one of the children is different. They may be so alike in appearance you can't identify baby pictures without other people in the frame, but you can distinguish their personalities with your eyes closed.

All our boys look like Hal, but they are all individuals. One faints at the sight of needles, another is sorry the doctor won't give him a turn giving shots to the younger siblings. One loves to be outside while another prefers to drape himself over the air conditioning vent. One agonizes over every decision, while another is happy to breeze through life on the wing.

They all have had one thing in common, though: they love to feel needed. One of the sweetest sights in life is a tiny little lad struggling under a load of groceries as he walks up the front sidewalk, "That's okay, Mom, I've got it. I don't want you to carry it." It takes an understanding Mom to let him labor up the steps himself because it's important to him.

"Thank you, son," she says. "That bag is heavy. I'm glad I have you to carry it in for me."

In a moment, the little shoulders widen, the stature increases a few inches, and he's ready to move a smallish mountain if it will help Mom. He finds the joy of fulfilling one of God's roles for his life—to be the man his family depends on.

God gives our sons the seeds of desire to carry out the role he's intended to play. A toddler will beam with happiness when he's asked to do a real job, even carrying a dirty diaper to throw away. The six- or seven-year-old begs to run the mower like his older brothers or Dad. There's something about real work, really being needed, that is much more satisfying than play.

When Melanie was about ten years old, her father was the manager of a knitting mill. The plant was dealing with a rush of orders and even her mom was pressed into helping out. Late one night Melanie was at the plant with her parents, her mom setting up the needles for the machine to knit a particular pattern. It looked kind of interesting to Melanie, so she asked her mom if she could do it. The equipment was practically unbreakable and whatever Melanie did could be checked and corrected if necessary, so she said yes. The task was actually pretty tedious and Melanie soon tired of it, but she was thrilled that she was putting together the program that would tell those big machines what to make. She felt like a part of the plant whirring and clanking around her, and it was real.

Our parents taught us to do real things at a young age. Hal's father taught him to build and refinish furniture and let him help with re-roofing and re-modeling jobs around the house. Melanie's parents brought her into the family business and gave her real tasks to do, running inventory, pricing merchandise, and helping clean the stores. Both families made sure we shared in the family's rewards—Hal's dad would share the payment when the customer picked up furniture, Melanie's folks would take the family out for doughnuts after a late-evening work session.

All children, but boys especially, want to contribute to the family. God has bade boys to one day support their families, to be the rock everyone clings to. Just like he drives his little Matchbox cars to work or pretends to be a soldier, he wants to do something real.

It's a good thing and can be a blessing to your family. How do you make it work?

An adage of industry and business is the thing that gets rewarded gets done. You have to be sure your sons get praised when they contribute something to the family. Hal chides husbands sometimes that they shouldn't expect bands to play and angels to sing when they fold a load of laundry, but wow, it ought to happen for the little boys in the house. "Thank you for putting that away, son. That really helps me. Everyone will be so glad to find their clothes in their drawers." Sure it's obvious, but he'll still be pleased you said it. It not only makes them feel appreciated, it focuses their attention on the purpose of the job—the contribution to the family and the service it gives to others.

It takes some investment of time and trouble to get them trained. If the parents are doing all the household chores because their sons can't do them "right," it's time to get the kids up to speed. Teaching and allowing them to take on more complex tasks can start earlier than many parents realize.

Our second son, Caleb, has been fascinated with cooking since he was a little guy. Melanie was nervous about him doing "real" cooking for the family, but a high-risk pregnancy changed her mind. Diagnosed with gestational diabetes, she couldn't eat the usual high-carbohydrate breakfast foods, and Hal was working long hours for a regional utility company which left little time for sleep, let alone additional household chores.

Enter Caleb, desperate to cook.

We worked out a plan where Caleb would get up with Hal and cook breakfast for Melanie while Hal was getting ready for work. Caleb was delighted and began experimenting with various omelets to tempt her appetite. Some were ... *interesting* ... but many were absolutely delicious. He really stepped in and saved the situation: Melanie was able to eat better for the baby's sake, Hal didn't lose even more sleep, and Caleb was able to make a serious difference to the family.

What's more, he got so adept at omelet making he took the show on the road to the 4-H district competition that year.

What if they can't do it right? Well, Caleb didn't present many perfect omelets at first. Some were overcooked — a personal horror for Melanie — some had strange fillings, and some were torn up in the cooking or serving. Still, Melanie thanked him every single time, then *later* — not at that moment — she offered suggestions how to improve the next day's effort, or praised specific improvements in the breakfast *du jour.*

We can afford to ruin a lot of cakes, turn a lot of underwear pink, or buy *way* too much spray cleaner if it helps our sons develop skills to better serve the family. The time and occasional expense we "waste" teaching them are an investment in the efficient running of our home — and theirs, one day.

Boys can contribute in meaningful ways as they begin to be old enough to work outside the home. We're not talking about Depression-era, all-hands-on-deck sort of work, necessarily. Melanie's grandfather and his twin brother were born in 1920. When they reached the eighth grade in school, Roosevelt was in office and the economy was in the doldrums. Their father announced they'd draw straws; one boy would continue on to high school, he said, and the other would go to work at the cotton mill. "And

I *won!*" recalls her grandfather, who became one of the most talented, self-educated mechanics in the textile business there.

Your family's budget may not need the income of a young teenager, but the boys can contribute in other ways. If you own your own business or manage one for somebody else, your sons can do many things that advance the mission: cleaning, sorting, clerical work and shipping tasks. Our sons help maintain our family's computers and business websites and run errands for the business. A pastor's son may help edit the church bulletin, update the outdoor signage, or help the deacons maintain the facilities. A consultant or salesman might take a son along on business trips as a driver, aide, or simply for company. It means a lot for the son to be a contributor, even if you can't afford to pay him directly.

There are times when the family really does need every financial boost it can garner. We have friends whose business is very cyclical in nature, and economic bumps have a disproportionate effect on their income. When your children are able and have a desire to help the family budget, it may be tempting to turn them aside; we want to provide them with everything they need, and let them keep whatever they earn. Resist the temptation. By sharing the family burden, they gain a sense of their own productivity, and they can experience the joy of blessing the family.

Our most recent child was born with a serious heart problem, and we spent several weeks in the intensive care unit while her condition was stabilized. The medical bills were outrageous and money was extremely tight. Dining out was not an option. Still, when the boys' history projects won statewide recognition, we decided to stretch the budget so they could attend the history club's celebration at a local pizzeria. When Melanie announced, in spite of some anxiety, that they'd be joining the group, there was great joy — then murmuring in the back of the van. Caleb and Matthew, the two oldest boys at home, got Melanie's attention and said, "Mom, we want to pay our way to make it easier for the family. We both have some money set aside and we really want to do this."

Melanie thought about refusing, but they were earnest about it. When she said yes, the amount left didn't seem quite as extravagant, and she felt a burden lifted. Can you imagine the feeling those young men had when they saw their mother's face go from worried to relaxed at that moment?

Over the years, our children have enjoyed treating the family to special things with their "own money." They've bought ice cream at the grocery store — even a young child can often afford a $2.50 half gallon, and his siblings' happiness will go a long way to teaching him the joy of sharing with the family instead of hoarding for himself. They enjoy combing the grocery salvage store for fancy jellies or European candy marked down for clearance. The amount of money they spend is less of an issue than showing them they can bless others with their labor and resources.

Encouraging this attitude in our sons will pay off in character when they are on their own — or even before. One family we know has suffered great financial reverses in the past few years; their family business is in an industry that came to a near stop, and the father developed health problems that further hindered his work. Their teenaged sons all got jobs and brought their earnings to their parents to pay utility bills and buy groceries.

Some folks would feel sorry for the poor kids giving up their free time to work, denying themselves all the fun they could have had with that money. Somehow, it's doubtful Christ would share that perspective. These boys are honoring their parents with their time and money, contributing to the home that raised them, and we think the Lord is pleased. May our sons facing such tests come out with such character!

Part Two

Civilization for the Tough

L ast year we took our son John Calvin on the obligatory tour of college campuses, known locally as "The I-85 Crawl" for the number of universities along that highway corridor. The most prestigious private school in the state is probably Davidson University, north of Charlotte. John's grades and scores had been good and we thought he might have a good chance at a top flight school like that, so we scheduled a visit.

Davidson is generally known as North Carolina's answer to the Ivy League, and some of its customs are intentionally similar to those at schools like Princeton. One we found intriguing is the free student laundry — all the washing is provided at no charge.

It was instituted at the request of the faculty nearly a century ago, we were told. Students at the then-all-male school were becoming too casual about the state of their clothing since there were no women around campus to impress. The professors earnestly entreated the administration to do *something* to make the classroom environment more ... *amenable* ... in those pre-airconditioning days.

Hence, free laundry to this day.

Do you ever look around your house and feel a need for some free laundry and a few other things? The boys' room looks like a tornado in a thrift shop and smells of feet and armpits.[1] We're not even going to talk about the state of their bathroom. The young men who are supposed to be doing school are having an arm-wrestling match and the others are having a burping contest. No one is wearing clean clothes, and they'd swear they don't have any; it's probably true considering you pulled 23 dirty sweat socks out of one bed this morning.

Mmm hmm, we are *real men* here! Hoo-ey!

Is this what raising a real man is all about? No! Raising manly men doesn't mean raising barbarians. Men can and should be civilized.

How can we teach our sons the things they will need to interact in society, to lead their families, to serve God? Step by step, suiting the way God made them, in an intentional, thoughtful way ... just the way we teach them everything.

Cleanliness of mind, body, and surroundings is a constant struggle. The effort to maintain purity of thought and avoid sexual sin is a never-ending battle that every man, down to our little boys, has to fight. We need to equip our sons for that war against sin, while preparing them to seek a wife and be a loving husband. We have to strengthen them to say "No," in order to bless the time when they can say, "Yes."

Now, cleanliness of surroundings is a fight they'd just as soon desert. Ever met a boy who lives to do laundry and loves to clean house? Nope, us neither. Does that mean they shouldn't be doing these things? Let's talk about it.

Can a boy who loves to belch and eats like an industrial vacuum learn to wear a tux at a formal banquet without losing one ounce of manliness nor killing his parents with embarrassment? Sure. Let's see how.

Is there any hope for a boy who can't keep a nickel in his pocket? Or the one who saves for years to buy the most powerful consumer computer made and then uses it for nothing but games and email? Can guys like that learn to manage their own family's funds? They can.

And what about that little boy who spends three hours on math and acts like sitting still is going to kill him? Can you find a way to homeschool him without both of you snatching yourselves bald-headed? It's been done. Well, mostly, anyway, and you can do it, too.

None of that will make any difference to us, though, if our sons don't learn to serve the Lord. The goal is not to raise well-mannered heathen. How can we reach his boyish heart and inspire in him a desire to be the Lord's man?

In the first part of this book, we talked a lot about the things boys do naturally that drive us crazy ... unless and until they are molded and shaped into the manly virtues.

Now we are going to talk about the things we want boys to do that drive them crazy ... unless and until we help them see the purposes, the goals, and the principles involved.

Once a boy grasps the why, once he's sold on the purpose, he will amaze you in his abilities and manliness. He's going to become a fine young man, you'll see.

Notes

1 In the movie *Amazing Grace*, William Wilberforce's uncle states that bachelors die in "rooms smelling of feet and armpits." We have become fond of quoting this to our sons when their room needs cleaning.

8

First Things

How blessed the man who does not walk
Where wicked men would guide his feet,
Nor stands in paths with sinful men
Nor sits upon the scorner's seat.
Jehovah's law is his delight,
His meditation both day and night.[1]

This book is written from a Christian perspective, and we've tried to illustrate as often as possible how we've applied the Bible in our family's day to day lives. It's a principle in our home that we try to bring Scripture to bear in any situation so that our children are saturated in a Biblical worldview. We discuss it with them, point it out to them, and make sure they know we're looking to God's word. What we call the basic commandment for homeschoolers is Deuteronomy 6:4-7:

> *Hear, O Israel: The Lord our God, the Lord is one! You shall love the Lord your God with all your heart, with all your soul, and with all your strength. And these words which I command you today shall be in your heart. You shall teach them diligently to your children, and shall talk of them when you sit in your house, when you walk by the way, when you lie down, and when you rise up.*

Our sons are blessed to grow up in a Christian home, under the teaching and example of Christian parents – not that either is perfect, but that both are forgiven and seeking to grow. We have friends who grew up in non-Christian homes, whether they were saved as adults or met the Lord through Bible camps or a children's outreach program. Often they seem to struggle with concepts and words and ideas that our children have heard from birth, principles that are familiar and comfortable to people who grew up in the church. While the boys are blessed to be surrounded by Christian testimony from their birth, it doesn't save a one of them.

The fact they're homeschooled with Christian-oriented text-books and daily devotions doesn't save them either. Their Christian heritage doesn't, nor their attendance at a good church. Each of them has to come to terms with God's command to repent and believe for themselves. Only God can change their hearts, and for that mercy we pray and witness and admonish them. We've seen the pain of enough families whose children brought up in Christian circles suddenly fell into disbelief, unwed pregnancy, drug use, or divorce. We just can't assume everything will turn out for the best just because they were in the best circumstances at the beginning.

If we don't take the time and effort to teach our sons about God, and Christ, and sin, and redemption, and sanctification, then we have failed them miserably. By God's grace they may be saved through other influences, but the gift of a Christian home will be of no assistance to them if we don't make it so.

Unfortunately, there is also no special checklist that we can follow that will ensure that our children come to Christ. Our goals are that our children would be without excuse and that we would be without regrets. We want to make sure there is never a question that they've heard the way to God's forgiveness, whether they embrace it or reject it.

In Your Heart

The most important effort we can make for our boy's spiritual health is to live the Christian life day to day and hour to hour. That's the pattern of Deuteronomy 6. But notice the first part of that passage – the word of God in your heart. You can't possibly live as a Christian before your children if you're not sure you know the Lord yourself. Boys are very sensitive to hypocrisy and they deeply desire to know their leaders are worthy of leading, that they believe and live what they say they do.

While the Bible has enough mystery and doctrine to keep a saint busy through this life and the next, the basics of faith and salvation are amazingly simple. Accept God's verdict that all of us have fallen short of His commandments and we are all in a state of rebellion against Him, a very good King.[2] The only possible sentence we can receive is final and eternal separation from God and any goodness He provides, which of course is *any* goodness whatsoever.[3] Our only option is to appeal to the court of God's judgment for the only relief available – a substitute to bear the punishment in our place.[4] Jesus, being the sinless Son of God, is the only man who doesn't have his own sentence to serve out; Christ is therefore the only one with righteousness to apply to our behalf.[5] When we invest our entire trust and hope in His forgiveness, abandoning any thought of earning our forgiveness from God,[6] then we rebels receive the King's pardon, a new heart, and His Holy Spirit. We also become members of His family – and disciples of His Son.[7] At that point, we're finally able to live as Christians for our sons' example, because that's what we are.

Teach them diligently

The second part shows us how to teach the things of God to our children: in the course of everyday life. Real discipling happens as our children watch us confront life on a daily basis making decisions based on the Word of God *and* explaining our reasoning to them. When we decide to unload all the children from the van and go back inside the store because we realize we received too much change, explaining that keeping the extra change would be stealing and breaking one of the Ten Commandments, our children see how seriously we take the Word of God. When we lose our temper and discipline someone unjustly or speak too harshly to our son, if we apologize and ask their forgiveness, they understand what repentance is and why we mean it when we say we are sinners saved by grace alone. Your example, especially when you don't realize anyone is watching, is the most powerful sermon you can preach your children, especially when you've pointed out why you behave the way you do.

Part of the teaching mentioned in Deuteronomy 6 goes beyond example, though. You've got to tell your children your heart and explicitly teach the Bible to them or they won't have a real example to follow. Like we said, good works never saved anyone. We decided many years ago to have devotions during our homeschooling time every day and family devotions in the evening. Hal has always told Melanie, "If you don't have time for devotions, you don't have time for school." We've found that to be true – there's almost no point in school without getting our hearts right first. Now that Hal is working at home, we can meet all together in the morning for one extended time. Whatever time of day you choose, the most important part of a family time of worship is doing it. It's far better that you worship with your children every day for a few minutes instead of doing an hour and a half marathon and then not getting around to it again for weeks afterward. Even if we do that, it's important to have the humility to begin again, as many times as we need to, recognizing that we stumble but there is One to lift us up again.

It is so important that our sons understand how to teach their own children the Word of God. Years ago, we heard Gregg Harris teach about how easily a Christian heritage is lost. The first generation loves God and does right, so they teach the next generation to do right, but maybe they neglect to explain why they do it. The second generation may teach their children to do right but they can't explain why. The third generation has no idea why their parents did things, so they seek their own path. Harris explained it much better than that, but the crucial part is passing on the gospel and the teachings of Scripture, not just a checklist of rules of behavior.

To do that, we keep things pretty simple. We choose a book of the Bible to read through, alternating types of books (a historical book from the Old Testament might be followed by one of the Gospels, then a section of the Psalms or one of the prophets, for example). Each day we read a short passage and explain it to our children. An excellent example of how to do this is J.C. Ryle's *Expository Thoughts on the Gospels*, a set of commentaries on Matthew, Mark, Luke, and John. The title looks forbidding, but Ryle, a conservative Anglican bishop at the end of the 1800's, writes in a very clear, winsome style. Reading through the commentaries gives you a good idea of how much to cover and how to draw meaning from the passage at hand.

We'll also choose a "hymn of the week," our plan to teach our children the hymns and spiritual songs. Each week we'll choose a hymn to sing all the way through each day, explaining the meaning of one verse each day. The old hymnbooks are full of encouragement and teaching, and we need to help our sons learn to worship with their minds, not just follow the music, when they sing.

We work on memorizing verses and longer passages of Scripture, and we've also used a simple catechism to give them a doctrinal framework to hang them on. Catechisms are an old teaching tool – one might say they were the FAQs of the church, since they are written in a question-and-answer format. *A Catechism for Boys and Girls*, which we use, begins very simply:

> Q: *Who made you?*
> A: *God made me.*
> Q: *What else did God make?*
> A: *God made all things.*
> Q: *Why did God make you and all things?*
> A: *For His own glory.*

Even three- and four-year-olds can handle that.[8]

Most denominations have some form of doctrinal statement like this to memorize or at least become familiar with, and many are available for downloading online at no cost. Whatever version your sons learn, whether the children's edition or the more complex adult catechisms, they're useful tools to help explain the faith to them and set certain principles in their minds.

We also pray, discussing prayer requests, with each person taking a turn and praying out loud. It's good to keep a prayer list, not just to make sure you remember who and what you're praying about, but also to keep notes on how God has answered. It's also good to keep an alert ear to how the boys pray; it's too easy to slip into rote phrases that don't really reflect the state of their hearts. We need to be careful of the same thing; prayer is a conversation with the living God, not a recitation or spell we're casting.

This is an investment in our sons' future, as well. We believe it's important that a man be comfortable reading the Bible, drawing basic applications from what he finds there, and that he be able to pray extemporaneously in groups. It's part of his role as a leader in the family as well as the community and church. Who will teach our grandchildren if we let this generation slip away or fall silent?

As You Walk in the Way

Beyond formal teaching, we teach our children as things come up. Any group of children will eventually disclose a tattletale in the bunch. We were blessed to find an illustrated poster called *The Brother Offended Checklist*, published by Doorposts.[9] Using it as a teaching tool, we've been able to teach our children the expectation that an offended believer should seek to restore the relationship someone else has broken. "Mama, my brother did —" is usually met with the countersign, "Have you talked to him about it?" We remind them that Matthew 18 teaches the need to go to the offender privately first, before bringing the authorities into the dispute. Responding to real situations with Biblical advice and Biblical words shows our children how to apply Scripture to their daily lives.

One caution that we've had to apply to ourselves as well as the children is that if we expect our sons to take the Bible seriously, we need to hold them and ourselves to a high standard. We don't allow jokes, puns, or clever turns of phrase using the words of Scripture, or for that matter, the words or tunes of hymns. This may be difficult, because if our children are raised up steeped in Scriptural language and spiritual songs, those will be the familiar phrases and tunes that come to mind when they feel silly. Frankly, sometimes the church is no help here; how many church nurseries have we seen with a sign in the baby area that says "We shall not all sleep but we shall all be changed,"[10] as if Jesus won't mind us lampooning His glorious return to make a

cute decoration by the diaper table? True, Jesus and the prophets used sarcasm on occasion, but we who aren't speaking the
inspired word of God need to be careful we don't undermine the
authority of the written word.

We probably made an error with our older sons when we
thought it would be good to explain our decisions and directions
as much as we did. Our hope was to gain their minds and wills,
not just their compliance. Likely, most parents who've gone this
route could tell you it tends to breed contempt, as if obedience
isn't necessary until agreement is reached.

> Mom: *"Son, get out of the street!"*
> Son: *"Why?"*

Write your own ending.

Now we don't explain ourselves to our children every time or
even most of the time, but it is still important that they learn
why certain rules are made and why certain decisions have to
happen. Our rule now is "Obey first, then ask me why, and I'll
be glad to explain." That's when you find out who really wants
to understand, and who was just stalling for time. It's a difficult
balance to strike, but so worthwhile.

Try and make spiritual topics a common, familiar subject of
conversation. Garrison Keillor wrote in one of his "Lake Wobegon"
stories about a father who had two special voices, one he used in
speaking about GOD, and one when speaking about MONEY. It's a
sign of discomfort, not reverence. After all, when the King James
Version speaks of God as "Thou," it's a familiar form of address,
not a formal one.[11] The old translation addresses God like a family member, though One due incredible respect. We are spiritual
people, citizens of a heavenly kingdom, and there is no need for
a tricked-up, phony-baloney kind of *awesomeness* when we talk

about the real life — here and hereafter — that we're living. God wants a true humility before Him, not a well-acted role-play.

Still, there are times that spiritual subjects can get personal. They should. God has a way of getting into things that we'd rather keep hidden from everybody, which should tell us it's time to dig into them first. Driving, working, or doing some other task together may be opportunities to broach potentially uncomfortable subjects. A casual question like, "How's your relationship with the Lord, son?" or "What have you been reading in your devotions lately?" can open up a conversation that will let you know what's going on in his heart. It can give you a chance to encourage him in the things of the Lord. Just remember our children can see right through us. They can handle flawed parents who are trying to give them a hand up, but a hypocrite who puts on the Righteous Face to put a struggling boy in his place won't win or keep their hearts for long.

We can't do anything that will ensure the salvation of our children – that's God's business. However, we can do lots to make sure that they know the good news, see the Christian life lived out, know that we truly believe what we are telling them. That way we'll have no regrets, and Lord willing, neither will they.

Notes for Chapter 8

[1] Psalm 1, first stanza, from *The Book of Psalms for Singing*

[2] Romans 3:10-12

[3] Matthew 7:21-23; James 1:17

[4] 1 Timothy 2:5-6

[5] Isaiah 53:4-6; John 14:6; 2 Corinthians 5:21

[6] Ephesians 2:8-10

[7] Romans 8:1-18

[8] You can read the entire catechism with Scripture references on the website of the Southern Baptist Founders Conference, http://www.founders.org/library/childcat.html. It is also included in Dr. Tom Nettles' *Teaching Truth, Training Hearts: The Study of Catechisms in Baptist Life* (Calvary Press, 1998).

[9] Pam Forster, *The Brother Offended Checklist: What To Tell A Tattletale*, published by Doorposts, 5905 Lookingglass Drive, Gaston, OR 97119 (http://www.doorposts.com)

[10] 1 Corinthians 15:51; 2 Corinthians 5:17

[11] English has lost distinctions other languages retain. Germans, for example, can be quite strict about who is allowed to address them in a friendly manner, *du*—like the old English "thou"—and the rest of the world, which is expected to maintain its distance as *Sie*. They even have a term, *duzen*, which refers to that permission to be familiar with one another. One of Hal's professors in college kept up correspondence with a persecuted Christian counterpart behind the Iron Curtain for *seven years* before the German decided it was probably all right for them to *duzen* each other. The German Bible uses *Du* to address the Almighty.

9

A Faithful Steward

"Old boys have their playthings as well as young ones; the difference is only in the price." Thus spake Poor Richard, in Benjamin Franklin's famous *Almanack*. Franklin, a man who made frugality one of thirteen virtues he systematically cultivated in himself, understood very well how easily distracted we are by the possession of a little bit of purchasing power. He wrote in his *Autobiography* of his chagrin as a boy when he overpaid a merchant for a toy whistle — an observation from the age of 79, and it still rankled.

When we were growing up, a child with birthday money was a danger to himself in a store; "the money was burning a hole in his pocket," anxious to be spent. Now the child is grown, and the presence or absence of cash isn't the issue — it's how much credit he can swing into action. The recent economic downturn, driven by a bursting bubble of home mortgages, is a major contraction of the credit available in our banking system, and it has *hurt.*

The implosion of banks, automakers, and the housing market has been driven by a basic abandonment of sound financial practice in the years before. Without pointing fingers at the prime movers of the crisis, it is simply true that if the failed businesses had run their affairs like a wise householder, much of this could have been avoided.

On the other hand, wise householders are hard to find these days.

Gary Smalley's useful book *If Only He Knew* includes the Holmes-Rahe Stress Test, a list of 43 stressful life events and their impact on our health: the death of a spouse is worst at 100, divorce is next at 73, and so on. Number 15 on the list is "change in financial status" — but 13 of the 14 situations ranked higher *also* have major financial implications.[1] No wonder we hear that estranged couples argue more about money than infidelity.

Cash, check, or credit?

Money is *not* "the root of all evils;" what the Bible says is "the love of money" is the root of all evil.[2] For most of us, it is a necessary part of life (those who aren't in prison or living on an island in a barter economy). But if the handling of it carries the possibility of disrupting our marriages, ruining our health, and wrecking the nation's economy, doesn't it make sense we need to teach our sons how to manage their money?

Not every parent does the job well. A young friend of ours who was away at college decided to do some Christmas shopping. She drove over to her bank and asked how much money she had in her checking account. She then drove all over town, buying a gift in this shop, then that, writing a check for $5 here and $7 there. A few days later she started getting angry phone calls from stores saying that her checks had bounced. She called her parents in tears,

"How could this have happened? I didn't spend as much as the bank told me I had!"

She had not understood that she needed to subtract any outstanding checks from her bank balance before spending the remaining money. She was charged hundreds of dollars in bounced check fees. It was a very painful and very expensive lesson learned.

Her family was very surprised that she didn't understand such a basic concept, yet who did they think was going to teach her? The schools might not teach you to balance your checking account. A lot of parents don't. We can do differently. This is an area where we can teach our children responsibility way beyond the norm.

Melanie's parents did an outstanding job with this. They were small business owners and their whole livelihood depended on their credit rating and financial reliability. When Melanie was thirteen, they opened a checking account for her — a rarity in those days. For the first couple of years, her parents were cosigners on the account and carefully taught her how to manage it and supervised how she used it. By the time she turned 15, she was free to use it like an adult — an eye-popper to local merchants.

We have done something similar with our sons, opening accounts for them with our local credit union. We teach them how the banking system handles check processing and tell them the secret lives of checking accounts. We make sure they understand what their available balance really is and how to avoid spending money they've already spent; we show them how to make deposits at the bank or from home, how to transfer money between savings and checking — everything they need to know about banking.

It says something about changes in banking that banking institutions don't seem nearly as cautious about initiating young people — as early as grade school years — into the financial system.

In a credit-driven economy, it's critical our sons know how to handle plastic. Last year there were several news stories about how college students are being sucked into credit card marketing schemes on campus; once they get the free promotional T-shirt or stadium blanket, they run up a balance, pay minimums each month, and graduate with $20,000 in consumer debt. Bad start to life, dude.

In our own family, we've used credit cards freely as an alternative to checks, but the rule has always been to pay the entire balance every month. If we ever fail to do so — it's happened a couple of times in two decades of marriage — then the use of credit stops until the balance is cleared up. Using credit cards can be a great convenience but paying credit card interest is a losing proposition from day one.

In the Internet economy of our children's generation, it is very difficult to manage without a credit card — as many of their parents have found trying to travel on business with cash and checkbook only. Like the checking account, we've used a graduated approach to teach our sons how to use these powerful and dangerous little cards properly. When they hit 14 or 15 — the approach of driving age is a good cue — we request a credit card in their name for one of our accounts and go through the same instructional process we did with checkbooks. They pay for gas at the pump; we send them on errands and get them to order things for us online. By using credit cards under close supervision for several years, they are not seduced by the exciting prospect of having a grown-up credit card. Knowing they will face the bill in a couple of weeks rather than deferring payments to an undetermined future takes away a lot of the temptation to overspend if they use plastic instead of cash.

A side benefit is that with most credit card companies this pattern of careful use and payment will show up on your child's credit report as a positive. It doesn't work as well if the parents don't manage their own cards well, though — your example can not only lead your child the wrong way, but will go on his record, too. Wise and cautious use while avoiding debt is the goal with credit cards — no matter who carries them.

Where should it go? Where did it?

We read a lot about marriage and family life while we were courting. One author who was very good about handling disagreements was a bit vague on money; his advice was to give a tenth, save a tenth, and spend the rest. That's more plan than a lot of couples have, but it left 80% of the resources unguided. The book we found most helpful then was Larry Burkett's *Your Money In Changing Times* because he went through and suggested proportions for all household expenses — what's reasonable and sustainable for mortgage, insurance, groceries, and so forth.

Based on our experience, which pretty much confirmed Burkett's recommendations, we teach the boys about the need for tithing and the inevitability of taxes. Students obviously don't worry about many of the categories, but knowing they exist prepares them for later.

Our first few years we kept our financial records by hand in a big book of accounting forms. Nowadays we keep it on the computer — we use *Quicken* and show the boys how to use it too — but the important thing is to track what they spend in enough detail they can review it later. Where did the money go? A couple of dollars on coffee or a soft drink is no big deal until you look back over the month and see $45 gone to that category. It helps them see why their parents are a bit stick-in-the-mud about stopping for a convenience store snack for our family of ten.

Entering the work world

We had different experiences with allowances growing up. Hal received a small allowance for many years until he was old enough to get an after-school job; it was small enough he had to save two weeks' worth to even buy a plastic airplane model, so mowing and raking yards was a pretty attractive option for spending money. Melanie's parents never gave her a separate allowance; she and her brother were part of the family business with their parents, and her folks bought her what she needed as her share of the family's financial blessings. She too was encouraged to do extra paid work within the business or look for a job if she wanted money of her own.

We've done a bit of both, giving an allowance for some times but sometimes not being in a position to do so even if we wanted to while getting our own business going. As our boys got older and wanted more money than they could save from relatives' birthday presents, we encouraged them to find part-time jobs or start their own micro-businesses.

That's been more challenging for us than most families because we travel a lot for business or ministry, and in the summers, we will often relocate our home office somewhere else, where we can continue working remotely.

The boys have managed to find some interesting opportunities to fit our family life, though. For several years, one of our sons made very good money working as a contract cleaner at a mega-church — that's right, he was a janitor. His friends couldn't believe he pushed a vacuum and cleaned toilets. Our son couldn't believe they worked fast food jobs for a third of the pay he got!

This turned out to be an almost ideal job for a family like ours. He could do his cleaning any time after Wednesday night prayer meeting and before Sunday morning. He frequently brought a younger brother with him to keep him company and to help out some, which built some very special relationships. It was only a once-per-week engagement but the hourly pay was more than acceptable for a teenager.

Another flexible job our older guys found was as roustabouts for an entertainment company. Their employer provides games, amusements, tents and catering for company picnics and community events; the boys spend the day setting up inflatable ball pits and slides, running the carnival midway, erecting tents and all sorts of jobs. They've earned a reputation for being extremely hard workers who don't complain. The owner calls them when he has a booking and if they're available, they work. Like the cleaning job, the pay is better than flipping burgers, and it has the benefit of being outdoors and more physically demanding than standing in front of a grill or dishwashing sink all evening.

A different kind of opportunity emerged for our older son. As a high school senior, he began writing movie reviews for a journal published by a local think tank; as he proved himself, they began offering him investigative and news stories as well. Since he is majoring in politics and economics, the experience of writing in the field is a resumé-building opportunity that he's been able to continue during breaks and sometimes during the semester.

Even unpaid volunteer work can open doors to opportunities. One of our sons volunteered to help at our state homeschooling conference and got to work with one of the keynote speakers, the author of a popular curriculum we've used. They had such good conversations during the weekend that when the author needed a young assistant to help staff his sales booth, he thought of our son. This son now travels with the company on weekends, representing the publisher at conventions all over the country. He's treated on the same basis as adult employees and has continued to build a good reputation for himself and his family in the process.

Our older son's success has inspired his brothers to seek their own money-making opportunities. Our outdoorsy sons have been putting out flyers to get jobs cutting grass and doing yardwork. They've sold wreaths, washed windows, done lots of odd jobs for grandparents. They are realizing that it is up to them to earn the things they want that go beyond their needs and not only that, but to prepare for the future. A son told me this week that he needed to be working more this summer because he wanted to save for college.

It is a good thing for boys to be looking forward like that. They will one day provide for their families and it will be such a blessing to their wives and children if they are planning ahead financially.

Looking Ahead

There are other financial transactions beyond just getting and spending. We adults may forget, after so many years and so many times, that the first attempt to handle all the financial complications of life can be daunting. It pays to take the same step-by-step approach we did with banking and credit. The first year or two our oldest had to pay federal taxes, Melanie, the family bookkeeper, worked out the return with him sitting next to her. This year, they did it together due to the added complications of income in two states and scholarships to claim. Next year, he'll be expected to fill out his own return with some checking from Melanie. After that, he should be on his own with an occasional call home to answer questions.

Larry Burkett's book was our personal assistant two decades ago and gave us a good start as a couple. The Biblical principles don't change but the financial world does, so it's a good idea to find current counselors to be sure your information is up to date. Last year our whole family took part in Dave Ramsey's *Financial Peace University* at our church. It was fantastic — an orderly, thoughtful, step-by-step guide to finances. His teaching on debt, budgeting, saving, and much more was spot on, in our opinion, and the DVDs were engaging and entertaining to watch. Although the program is aimed at adults, we chose it over those supposedly relevant to teens. The boys need to start thinking long term about finances, not just about how to best spend the little bit they have available now. Our sons came away extremely motivated to avoid debt, work hard and plan for the future.

James Herriot's books about his career as a Yorkshire veterinarian describe the early bachelor days when he and his employer shared a house. The veterinary practice's cash account was kept in a beer mug on the mantel, crumpled pound notes overflowing onto the hearth rug below. It seemed adequate at the time, though the bookkeeper they hired later on was properly horrified.

That kind of casual, agnostic approach to money won't work for our sons. We have to be sure they understand what they're dealing with, so they will control their finances and not be controlled by them instead. In the process they'll learn a lot more than balancing a checkbook. They can learn not to be greedy or self-indulgent by examining what they are spending and asking why. They learn to be diligent and uncomplaining by working hard at difficult and sometimes unpleasant jobs. They learn self-control by working hard, waiting for their pay, then saving for something special. They learn prudence by saving for emergencies. They'll learn to be faithful in little things like record keeping the first year they have to estimate high on their taxes because they couldn't prove expenses. They learn the importance of a good reputation when their hard work earns a call for another job, while a friend is passed over.

Conclusion

Finally, if we prepare our sons well for the role of providing for their families, we will bless them and future generations. It will lift a load of care from our own aging shoulders, too. Parents share in their children's worries, and when we think of our own parents' concern during our lean times, we can't imagine what their burden would have been if they had not prepared us to avoid debt and bad decisions.

It's not really important to us whether our sons are wealthy or poor, so long as they are faithful to the Lord's calling on their lives. Whichever way they go, though, we want to make sure they are fully equipped to deal with abundance or want, and are not suffering from poor judgment or inadequate preparation. As we give them opportunities to grow and mature with the benefit of our good counsel (and perhaps our experience of bad counsel), we'll be doing our part to make that happen.

NOTES FOR CHAPTER 9

[1] Gary Smalley, *If Only He Knew: Understanding Your Wife* (Grand Rapids, MI: Zondervan, 1982), p. 126.

[2] 1 Timothy 6:10 (KJV). Most modern translations say *the love of money is the root of all kinds of evil.*

10

Your Own School for Boys

Our boys always seem to hit a challenging period when they're nine. It came as a surprise when our oldest son, the precocious reader who pleaded to be homeschooled when he was four, suddenly fell off the horse with his school work when he turned nine. He became the Slowest Homeschooler in the West (or any other point on the compass, it felt like). A regular math lesson would last three hours. He was taking *forever* to finish just the usual daily requirements, and Melanie was about to the point of distraction with him.

One night we were listening to one of our favorite recordings, Gilbert and Sullivan's *The Pirates of Penzance*, and came to that wonderful patter, "The Major General's Song":

> *I am the very model of a modern Major-General,*
> *I've information vegetable, animal, and mineral,*
> *I know the kings of England, and I quote the fights historical*
> *From Marathon to Waterloo, in order categorical;*
> *I'm very well acquainted, too, with matters mathematical,*
> *I understand equations, both the simple and quadratical,*
> *About binomial theorem I'm teeming with a lot o' news,*
> *With many cheerful facts about the square of the hypotenuse.*
>
> *I'm very good at integral and differential calculus;*
> *I know the scientific names of beings animalculous:*

In short, in matters vegetable, animal, and mineral,
I am the very model of a modern Major-General.

What caught his ear that particular night we don't know, but after listening to that list of esoteric knowledge, John burst out, "I wish *I* knew all those things!"

Melanie, in one of those truth-filled moments born of exasperation, shot back, "You know, we'll be studying most of those things one day — that is, *if you ever get out of fourth grade!*"

"Wh ... wh ... what do you mean?" he asked. John had a slight stammer at the time, and the surprise of the moment brought it out.

Melanie explained that she could drag him through fourth grade math all right, but there was no way on earth she was going to be able to drag him all the way to differential calculus. If he really wanted to learn all those neat things, he had to start taking some responsibility for learning along the way. He had to stop dragging his feet and fighting her at every turn.

John asked her if she could give him a list of what he was expected to do the next day. She did, not expecting much from it.

She didn't know this was the start of something new. Behold, the following day John completed all his schoolwork, for the first time in months.

Melanie realized several things that day. She learned that boys really need a goal, some purpose for the day. She learned that giving them a list can help them see what has to be done and allow them to take charge of doing it. It also gives them hope that there really *is* an end to the school day, if they don't prolong it themselves.

Later, she learned that setting time limits and seeing that subjects which ran over the allotted time were finished during "free" time later in the day was very motivating. As the boys grew, she learned how to use their desire to compete with academics, letting them do drill work against the clock or race each other to finish math first, or finding opportunities for them to enter academic contests outside the home.

No matter how much mothers and sons may be alike, they are likely to be very different in some important ways that will really impact their homeschooling together.

Mothers who have girls before they have boys are sometimes in for a shock. "How in the world to you homeschool all those boys?" they ask. "I'm going crazy with *one*." Even an experienced home educator may feel like a failure, when it may be she was simply unprepared for the differences between teaching boys and girls.

Common generalizations may be misleading as well, which doesn't help. The first books we read about homeschooling, before we even had any children to teach, cautioned that boys developed more slowly than girls. It's okay, the authors said, if the boys aren't ready to read as soon as their sisters. Since we didn't have a test subject to compare this to, we took it on their authority. When we held our newborn son, we looked at each other and said, "Now, he's a boy, so remember his learning ability will probably develop slower than we think. And that's okay, we won't push him too hard."

So after years of carefully preparing ourselves to be very, very accepting of letting John develop at his own, deliberate pace, one day, just before he turned four, John (who didn't begin talking until he was two) came up to Melanie and said, "Mama, would you teach me how to read?" *He was three.* His friends from church, all a couple years older than him, were starting to homeschool, and he wanted to be part of it, too. Thinking that surely this was a passing fancy, Melanie started gently teaching him phonics the month he turned four. And by the end of the year, he was reading children's books on his own — it floored one of our mothers, a grade school librarian. It floored us, too.

After a few more early readers, we got the son God had prepared us for — bless his heart, he suffered from the family's tendency to dyslexia, and he didn't really learn to read until he was nine. Sure enough, we had settled back to thinking that maybe our early advisors were wrong, and we had a good curriculum that seemed to work really well with young readers. This son was as big a surprise, in his own way, as the first was. We praise God that with some wise counsel and lots more patience than we thought we had, we lived through that period and he is now reading very well and ahead of grade level.

It all demonstrates, once again, that God creates us as individuals, not as units of a particular class. Some boys learn slower than girls, but some don't. Some of the characteristics we've observed or been told about will apply to some boys, and others won't. Some of the ideas we've used successfully may not work as well for you, and some we rejected may be just the ticket for you and your sons. Take this advice like a watermelon — eat the part that's sweet, and spit out the seeds.

Developmental differences

All of that said, we *have* concluded that it's not really true that boys mature more slowly than girls. Rather, boys mature more quickly in certain areas, and girls in others. For example, boys tend to have a quicker grasp of spatial reasoning, like constructing a model out of building blocks, or estimating how many objects will fit into a certain size container.

Where we have challenges are in areas where they do develop more slowly. One critical example is small motor skills — like handwriting. Curricula that require a great deal of writing in early grades are often frustrating to young boys, while their sisters will happily fill out worksheet after worksheet. It may have been the perfect textbook for your daughter, but it may be perfectly *wrong* for your son.

Recently Melanie was talking with a mother whose son was dragging his feet in science. He liked the concepts fine, but he was having a terrible time answering questions in the text and doing the written tests. Melanie suggested that the mother give him the questions and tests orally, and record his answers herself. Is that cheating? The mother was concerned.

Our rationale is that sometimes the purpose of writing is *writing.* Obviously Mom can't be a substitute for penmanship exercises. If your student is practicing timed essays for college entrance exams, they need to be pushing pen over paper, and doing a lot of it. If that's a problem, it's one that has to be confronted and mastered. One of our sons struggles with long writing assignments, but to pass AP Biology he had to be able to carry out multiple timed essays on the exam. Biology isn't a writing course, but the format of the test required it, and he wrote *lots* that year.

But why hold back second- or third-graders in science or history or math just because they're behind on their language arts? Read to them, buy books on CD or mp3 formats, and help them with their writing; eventually they can catch up. Many boys just aren't developmentally ready to read and write in kindergarten or first grade, as some programs expect, but that shouldn't impede everything else.

Along the same lines, we're extremely skeptical of letting younger students use calculators for common math problems. Boys love

a technical gadget, of course, so they'll give you a hundred argu-
ments in favor of the practice. When a high schooler is working
out formulas in chemistry or physics, or when the math requires
numerous conversions and tables of information as in trigonom-
etry, then we use the calculator. At that level, it is just a tool to
speed up the higher-level problem solving which is the real focus.

In elementary grades though, where the students are learning basic computational skills, calculators are worse than a
crutch — they're like leaving the training wheels on their bicycles
until they're 18, then giving them a motorcycle for graduation. The
daughter of a friend came by our house one day for help with
her college algebra course. The professor was enamored of the
(then-new) graphing calculators, and everything in the course
had to be done with the machine. This student simply couldn't
figure out why she was adrift in a subject she knew she should
have understood. A few minutes talking with her made it clear
that she had never mastered the concept of x-y coordinates — a
torpedo in the side of a graphing calculator course!

That's a basic rule for us: Let them learn to handle the fun-
damental concepts before giving them the short cut. Obviously,
it's a rule that can help girls as well as boys!

Developmental "delays"

Granted there are differences, but what about developmental
delays? How do you handle sons who really seem overdue in
some areas?

Remember our shock when after our "success" at teaching our
first sons to read so easily, our dyslexic son arrived? In fact, we
found our sons — with the same parents, same family life, same
curriculum at first — learned to read fluently at ages that varied

four to five *years* from their brothers. That alone can be a key argument for considering homeschooling for boys, because reading ability is a key marker for placing children in institutional schools. If the third grade teacher assumes everyone is reading near the third grade level, it will be difficult for the slow readers to keep their place in school — never mind if they are excelling in math or science. In home education, it's no problem if the same child is in fourth grade math, third grade science, and still working through the second grade reader. They've got *years* left to catch up.

One thing we found encouraging was a history of Civil War chaplains written by a member of General Lee's staff, the Rev. J. William Jones. One of the duties of chaplains was visiting hospitals and camps, and many found large numbers of soldiers who had never learned to read. The book mentions many occasions where chaplains and soldiers worked together to teach these men letters, and report how frequently men who entered the service totally illiterate learned enough in a short time to read the Bible — at that time, the King James Version — for themselves.[1]

Confronted with this challenge, we determined a slow start reading was not going to hamper any of our sons' intellectual development. We read complex books aloud to the children, taking time to explain the hard parts. We buy books on CD to listen to in the car or at home. The science curriculum we use is available as mp3 audio files, which helps some of our sons. All these things allow our boys' comprehension to mature so when the technical ability to sound out words and read fluently catches up, they quickly race to grade level and beyond. And the flexibility of home education allows us to individualize each son's education according to his own strengths and needs — a great advantage for boys developing more quickly in one area than another.

Gender differences in learning

When our oldest son was considering colleges, we were looking for a strong liberal arts program with an outstanding economics department, one of his prospective majors. A guidebook and a friend recommended we look at Hampden-Sydney College, a historic, all-male school in Virginia (Patrick Henry's sons attended). We were suitably impressed with the college's academics and facilities and enjoyed meeting with the economics professors, but when John got to sit in one of the classes, he was *lit up* about the professor's manner when he returned.

"It was great, Mom!" he said. "The professor was calling the guys 'boneheads' and teasing them. He talked up a storm and even shouted a few times!"

Melanie's thought was, "And this is good *how?*" but John clearly loved the atmosphere there. The young men at the college also felt respect and affection for the professor, judging from what they posted online.

Research has shown there are distinct gender differences in the learning process. Dr. Leonard Sax of the National Association for Single-Sex Public Education has collected much of this research to highlight these differences. This was an area he singled out: while a young woman may have been intimidated or even felt assaulted by such vehemence in the classroom, young men ate it up.

How can we make our classrooms more boy-friendly? How can moms, who do most of the teaching, connect with their sons and give them a passion for scholarship? If we can successfully distinguish differences in learning from willful sin, won't we all be happier and more productive?

Louder, Mom

A common exchange in our house is the parent addressing a son who is engrossed in a book, or writing, or maintaining a steady pulse rate — *anything*. No answer leads to a louder call, then finally one tinged with exasperation.

"Son, are you *deaf?*"

Son looks up, blinking, like one just awakened.

"Sorry, I didn't hear you," he says.

Oddly enough, he probably *didn't*. Boys don't hear as well as girls, generally, and especially tones in human speech. It's like the Lord hard-wired girls to listen to people and deal with relationships — nobody understands a baby's cry like a mother — while boys are wired to ignore distractions and concentrate.

It carries through to adulthood. One of our favorite movies is *The Incredibles*. In an early scene, Bob (secretly "Mr. Incredible") comes home burdened with problems at work. His children are going wild at the dinner table, but Bob is deep in his own thoughts. Wife Helen, struggling unsuccessfully to rein in the children, finally shouts, "Bob! It is *time* to *engage!*" Hal admits that when he is focusing on a project, the house could probably burn down around him; if a child speaks to him and he doesn't raise his eyes from the computer, whatever the child said — even if Dad responded — was totally unrecorded by his brain. Mr. Incredible is painfully funny because he is so *real*.

This becomes a problem when it is time for our sons to engage their schoolwork and the boys have classified our voices as distractions. Shields up, full power! We can't lower the expectation that our sons listen for our call and respond quickly, but maybe we need to speak more loudly at the start to get their attention.

Paradoxically, the opposite problem can also be an issue. If God designed our sons to concentrate, it should come as no surprise if they prove remarkably distractable. We have one son whose mind will wander in the middle of a question.

"Mom, I'm not sure how to set up this long division problem with — did you see that bird?" he'll say.

"Aargghh," thinks Mama.

Is it possible to hold a boy's attention? Yes, but it may take more energy and noise and activity than you expect. If you talk to boys in a group, you have to speak loudly, with enthusiasm, if you aim to keep their minds with you. And if you speak softly, they may even talk over you, apologizing profusely when you rebuke them for interrupting.

"I'm sorry, Mom, I didn't hear you."

This is a great annoyance, yet in most cases, it isn't sin. It's a gender difference that we have to adjust for — whether the comparison is between the way to teach a girl or a boy, or whether it's simply Mom (female) getting across to Son (male). And there's no question it can be an adjustment for the girls who want everyone to speak softly! Perhaps these future moms of boys need to learn the differences too, so they can effectively reach their sons in the future.

There are other things besides hearing and concentration differences, of course. Our boys get cabin fever when they've been confined without exercise for a time due to bad weather, ill health, or long travel. They have a much tougher time settling down to their work in this situation. Melanie's been known to stop in the middle of a lesson and say, "Give me ten on the stairs," the indoor equivalent of Coach saying, "Gimme a lap." When they return, they're much calmer and find it easier to study.

It also helps to schedule the subjects that take the most concentration during the times distractions are least. One of our sons gets up earlier than anyone else because he found his math takes drastically less time if he can do it before the rest of the family is up.

That's pretty much the only time of day that's quiet, so we allow our guys to drown out the noise with music played softly or on headphones. We stipulate music without words and in accordance with our family's standards. They prefer classical music anyway, particularly movie scores that *Melanie* finds distracting (life is challenging enough without suspenseful background music building to a crisis).

We also encourage the older boys to work in different rooms than the one where Melanie is working with the younger ones. This can help them get more work done with less distraction — unless they create their own distractions talking to each other or goofing off while out of sight. If we catch them wasting time like that, they're back in the room with Mom for a while. They hate it — it's really hard to do pre-calculus while listening to grammar chants, a fussy baby, and an imaginary ambulance, all at the same time!

The funny thing is that sometimes the most distractable child is the one who is most distracting to everyone else! Our son who is most easily frustrated is never entirely still. If there is something within reach of his feet, he is sliding it around on the floor, kicking it, rocking it back and forth. If there's a song in his heart it comes out in a hum. He's got rhythm, expressed with tapping pencil. Annoying, it is, and he doesn't even notice himself. Just when Melanie is about to start tearing her hair in frustration, the boy fiercely shoves his own hair back and pleads, "Mom! Can you please make them be quiet? I can't concentrate!"

He's a sensitive young man and he's always awfully sorry when he realizes (is told) what he's been doing, but his parents have to struggle to keep their temper and just keep pointing out to him that he's making an unintentional racket. "You are responsible for whatever your body is doing," Hal tells him. He's getting better at recognizing what he's doing — call it self-awareness — but now one of his younger brothers is doing the same thing!

Thus the parents learn patience from their children ...

"I think he must be hyperactive..."

The natural level of activity of boys is a difficult thing for teachers to manage. The traditional classroom environment is set up for rows of young scholars, sitting quietly and attentively, drinking deep from the river of knowledge.

That doesn't seem like normal behavior for boys; like the dog trained to sit quietly with a treat balanced on its nose, some can be conditioned to it, but it doesn't come naturally. American literature is full of boy characters, the Tom Sawyers and Penrod Schofields, for whom the strictures of the schoolroom is a bondage worse than chains.

In his book *That Hideous Strength*, C.S. Lewis creates a world where crime is considered a medical disorder. One of the characters observes, with sadistic approval, that *punishment* of crime has an end, whereas *treatment* can continue indefinitely. Behavior which once was punished in school ("Go stand in the corner, young man!") is now "mercifully" treated with prescription drugs. After all, boys aren't just active, they're *hyper*active. It's not that they don't pay attention; they have a *deficit*, a *disorder*, and it cries out for treatment. They aren't *normal*.

So what's "normal" and who defines it? It's a great reason to consider homeschooling boys. We're convinced if our sons were in school, they'd be on so many pills they'd rattle when they walked. Yet they've learned quite well, they have many friends, and they get along pretty well in the community. Where's the problem?

We need to be careful that wherever our boys go to school, we don't bring the classroom expectations home with them. Teaching a typically wiggly young boy is a matter for patience, and especially because his behavior is so different from the girls. The girls' behavior, which is amply rewarded in the classroom, is the memory of young women teaching their first classes, and of mothers teaching their boys at home. It's what they expect.

It's true that boys are active. They're like cats, which are seldom really stationary; even at rest, their tails twitch. Boys seem to be in constant motion, and it makes it hard to even imagine, let alone believe, that they are thinking at all.

Henry Adams observed with quiet horror that Theodore Roosevelt was "pure act," constantly busy about something alarming, yet history shows Roosevelt had a rich intellectual life that accompanied his famous penchant for physical activity. We've found that boys *are* able to learn while moving, but we have to adapt our expectations to it. Mothers remember the admonition to study seated in a desk, feet flat on the floor, maintaining proper posture, with the light coming over the student's left shoulder. What she may find instead is her son does his best work standing up — incidentally, Thomas Jefferson did much of his writing at a standing desk — or spread out at the kitchen table rather than a school-type desk. He may listen to reading aloud lying upside down with his feet waving in the air.

Can your schoolroom tolerate this? It may be annoying to the teacher, but is it *wrong*? Why not give him the freedom to move, stretch, fidget, and flex, if that frees his mind to better comprehend?

Hal is capable of deep concentration. He has been known to focus so hard on a document that the motion-sensing light switch in his office suddenly plunges him into darkness. Even so, some projects drive him to a chalk board where he can make large arm motions, writing notes, diagrams, or formulas across a large space then step back to observe them. Some problems are best worked out while pacing around. Even squeezing a tennis ball may help work out the nervous energy so the brain can run smoothly. All of these may be a help to your sons as well.

"Why do I have to learn this, anyway?"

What are some other distinctions about teaching boys? One is the way they perceive the world of knowledge. Often they need more than facts, they need the principles and reasons which undergird them. Why is this fact important? What is the purpose for studying this material at all? Will it ever be useful, or are we just collecting data to archive in our brains?

This makes discussion of ideas paramount. They need to see through the plots of the books they read and discern the author's theme and message. They need to recognize the philosophy and worldview expressed in art and entertainment; when they understand there's more to the painting or music than the picture or melody, it becomes more relevant to them. How does the philosophy of the scientist or historian affect the work they do?

They need practical applications for the material they're learning, too. Hal often found courses in college which only seemed to prepare the student for the next class; the connection to life beyond the academy was seldom made clear. A mother asked him recently whether her son, who planned to study agriculture in college, really needed high school chemistry, since he didn't see a connection with his ultimate interest. Hal suggested she might look for people in real-world agriculture that could show him how principles in chemistry are used to test soil composition, to figure pesticide and fertilizer application, to medicate animals and optimize crop processing. A hammer is a more valuable tool when you recognize the existence of nails.

What's your goal, son?

Even at younger levels, you can give your boys real problems to solve. Use similar triangles to measure the height of trees in your yard. Let them figure out the surface area of a room — subtracting the area of windows and doors — before buying paint. Encourage them to apply basic economic principles to their business — how many yards will they be asked to rake if they do it for free, or if they charge $20? Challenge them to remember Bible verses or historical examples that apply to current events. Real world examples give your sons a handle on why they're learning these things.

What about subjects that don't have an obvious application, other than fulfilling a requirement somewhere? If you can't think of the real-world use of that subject, then look to your son's goals for motivation. "Son, what do you think you'd like to do for a living? Do you realize you'll need to learn this material in order to qualify for that training?" With younger students, it's not so important — *everything* requires more education than they've gotten so far.

Just like our eldest son and the Gilbert & Sullivan song, your sons need to understand that school is not something to live through and get past, but training and preparation for their future. It provides the building blocks for whatever God has planned for his life.

Boys respond well to short-term goals, too. They want to conquer things. They want to know there is an end that can be attained as well; one of the most discouraging sights to the westbound pioneers was the endless peaks of the Rockies and Sierras revealed as they struggled to the top of each new mountain. If a boy doesn't know what he is expected to do in a day, he may begin to ask himself, "Why finish math? Mom is just going to think up something else for me to do!" This can drag out the school day and breed frustration on all sides. Nagging results and schoolwork doesn't.

We found it very helpful to give the boys a list of the day's assignments and tell them they are free to go as soon as the list is complete—and not free at all for computer or recreational reading or going outside, until it is. Then you've made finishing school *his* problem—and his goal. It makes school something to be conquered.

Our boys like to figure out how much they have left before the end of the year. Our school calendar varies a great deal because we are often traveling or pursuing interesting opportunities which may take us away from the books for a while. Our rule, though, is that school is out when the books are done.

As long as a boy is not discouraged by a seemingly insurmountable task, a goal is extremely motivating. The more objective you can make the list, the less emotional it becomes. The less nagging and guilt come into the picture, the better it will work.

What a pleasure to have a young man get up early and announce mid-morning, "My schoolwork's done!"

The benefit of stress

Another interesting item from the research collected by Dr. Sax and others is that boys tend to learn better under stress. When a boy—or man—is concentrating hard, he often will bite his lip or stick out his tongue; it's a mild discomfort that seems to focus his thinking. It's another area where mothers and sons see things differently; moms naturally try to reduce stress, when it actually may be hampering progress.

Mom: "Here, Honey, you don't have to be timed on that worksheet. Take all the time you want."

Son: [Dies of boredom]

The stress of working against the deadline introduces competition back into the equation. It makes the task more interesting, more "profitable" in the boy's eyes.

There's another aspect to it. Melanie served as the testing coordinator for a large local homeschooling group. Year after year, she saw that most of the children scored much higher on conceptual math test than on the timed problems. While the accuracy and usefulness of standardized testing can be debated, the fact is our children will be subjected to them in school and beyond. We may be doing our sons a disservice by trying to make things easier for them. Perhaps they are better off working by the clock—both to motivate them now and to prepare them for later.

Never Send an S.O.S.

When they do find things difficult, boys (like their fathers) may be reluctant to ask for help. We parents need to be aware of this and try to anticipate it when it happens.

One of our goals is to train our children to become independent learners. By the high school years, we expect them to be in charge of their own day's activities and manage their day-to-day education. We tell them what to have done each day, or each week if they've been faithful, and to please come ask Mom or Dad if they have problems. The trap is that somehow they *never* have problems until we check up on them. With lots of younger children who need constant attention with school, it's hard to keep a close watch on the "independent" ones, and the big boys who assure us, "Yes, I did my math today" with the mental " ... as much as I could" may slide by until someone actually inspects their work. Occasionally we've found one who stumbled over a certain type of problem, then decided to bypass it and finish the rest ... for the rest of the year if they could get away with it. Even reminding them to check in with Mom at the end of the day is often forgotten in the press of busyness.

One option that helped is telling our boys to note the problem numbers that they couldn't do at the top of the page. When Melanie reviews their work, she can call them and go over those problems. No one had to ask for help!

With the upper level high schoolers, it's helpful to have progress meetings from time to time. "Let's talk about what you are studying in chemistry; bring me your book." This provokes discussion and helps uncover any misunderstandings they have.

If you develop independent learners, they will be able to seek out and teach themselves all kinds of subjects throughout their lives. If you teach them to ask for help or find assistance when they need it, they will do even better. Our eldest son, who had very seldom sat in any kind of classroom environment, had an easier adjustment to college than many of his friends from institutional schools. He was trained to manage his own studies and go back to the professor when he encountered difficulties; while his friends, used to constant monitoring, were adrift in the new independence of college academics.

Conclusion

Boys and girls are made by God to be different and that impacts how they learn and how they manage learning. Unfortunately, the majority of teachers, both in institutions and at home, are women who were raised in a feminist educational environment and have a hard time accepting the idea of gender differences, much less that boyish ways of learning and doing school aren't wrong or inferior, just different. It's so important to understand the interplay here between our own upbringing, education, and desires and what our boys need. Understanding that will make learning more of a pleasure for us and for our sons.

NOTES ON CHAPTER 10

[1] J. William Jones, *Christ in the Camp: or, Religion In Lee's Army* (Richmond, VA: B. F. Johnson & Co., 1887). Modern reprints are available.

11

CHIVALRY IS NOT DEAD

Recently we were guests at a formal dinner. It was a family event so there were several children present, and two young boys were sitting together with several adults at one table. The boys were wiggling in their seats, interrupting adults' conversations with childish remarks, playing games with their silverware and banging on the water glasses. They were just being boys, but their behavior was inappropriate for the situation.

Another time, Melanie was at an outdoor function with other homeschool families. Four boys of various ages walked into the park with their mother, carrying a cooler and a blanket. They spread the blanket out for a picnic, then sat down politely, just like their mother — propped on one arm with their legs together and stretched to one side. They were just being polite, but their body language was inappropriate for young men.

These are two extremes in the range of possibilities with boys and manners. Some people, often men, think sensitivity about etiquette is effete, affected, and only a suitable concern to old ladies. Others, often women, find the subject so crucial they will enforce aesthetic sensitivity on young men without recognizing their distinctiveness as *men*. The true path, like so much in life, is a balance that acknowledges the need for guidance to help sinful people get along, but does not make a destructive tyrant out of the resulting rules. True courtesy is a matter of consideration for others, and a worthwhile study for the Christian young man. And proper manners can, and should be, a manly virtue in themselves.

What the Bible Says About Manners

The classic illustration of "manners" in our culture is the question of which fork to use; it isn't addressed in Scripture that we've found. It's a cultural norm, the same as the question whether the fork should change hands; the American cuts his steak and transfers the fork back to his dominant hand, while the British or European diner holds the fork points-down throughout the meal. While visiting Saudi Arabia, Hal had to concentrate not to cross his legs or otherwise let the bottom of his shoe be visible to others. We committed an accidental faux pas when we gave a clock to a Chinese relative; in their culture, it is associated with death, which does not make it a cheerful birthday gift![1] All of these are rooted in local custom and don't show up in the Bible except as applications of a larger principle.

The basic Scriptural teaching on manners boils down to two precepts—consideration toward others and humility toward ourselves. Peter concluded his first Epistle with the call to be *of one mind, having compassion for one another; love as brothers,* be *tenderhearted,* be *courteous.*[2] Paul told the Romans to be *kindly affectionate to one another with brotherly love, in honor giving preference to one another.* He tells them to be humble: *Do not be wise in your own opinion,* he admonishes.[3] If we were consistent following just these principles, much of the rest would take care of itself.

But there are a number of passages that address matters we consider basic to proper behavior. The Bible has a great deal to say about our conversation, for example—not just in what we say but the manner in which we say it. We should be good listeners, first *swift to hear, slow to speak, slow to wrath.*[4] We are supposed to be humble about out own opinions and not cut off others mid-sentence to respond.[5] We are cautioned to moderate our criticism of others. When Paul instructs Titus that Christians are to *speak evil of no one,* the Greek term he uses is *blasphemeo,* which we would normally associate with slandering God. It also describes reviling, maligning, or slanderous speech toward our fellow men — think "character assassination."[6] We are not to mock the handicapped, play practical jokes on one another, or indulge in crude humor.[7] Books could be written on the warnings against gossip.

Other topics will be addressed separately, but always, the guiding principles are consideration and humility. This not only expresses respect and kindness toward others, it helps ensure that our message is not torpedoed by a perception of rudeness. In other words, the world has rejected our Master, and will be inclined to reject us as well; let's be sure that it is only because we are like Him, not because we manage to cause offense by our inattention or insensitivity.

Some Practical Examples

Back to the "which fork?" question — knowing the right behavior for formal situations is an important, career-enhancing social skill. Even in our merit-based society, proper grammar and correct table manners seem to mark a man's class at first meeting, so we've expected our children to learn both. Nearly every job interview Hal has attended, on either side of the table, included a fancy meal out, usually with a sharp-eyed manager looking at how the candidate handles social occasions. A candidate who ordered too many drinks from the bar or couldn't carry on a conversation over dinner was severely handicapped before the first formal interview.

Why would table manners be important in hiring a junior staff member? Because in the supposedly casual social environment over dinner, the guard is lowered and the employer can uncover a remarkable amount about the candidate. Will they represent the company well when we entertain customers or vendors? Or will they embarrass their supervisors in front of company officials? Are they discreet or foolish in social situations? Are they genial and easy to communicate with? The interview itself would indicate whether the man could do the job. The social interview, the dinner, would demonstrate whether he could do it congenially and whether he was promotable or not.

Recently a member of a prominent political family was suggested for appointment to fill a vacant seat in the Senate. The candidate staged a well-reported dinner meeting with a widely-known community activist. The elder man, a media-savvy veteran, wisely clasped his hands in front of his plate and never touched a fork while reporters were present. The candidate, however, nervously continued eating, pausing to swallow before answering reporters' questions. Sure enough, commentators observed the unfavorable contrast between the ease of the veteran and the discomfort of the "amateur." Did the candidate drop food on the table or talk with a mouth full of dinner? Not at all — it was simply a matter of how the candidate handled the demands of being "on stage," which was, "Not very well," in this instance. The unfavorable comparison did nothing to advance the candidate's cause, and ultimately the appointment went to another. Failing to teach our young men how to behave like gentlemen may similarly limit their sphere of opportunity.

That applies to more than job seeking and political campaigning. Melanie took a short-term missionary trip to Mexico when she was in college. One thing that was drilled into the team was the unusual hospitality being shown to the students. In that society, they were told, most entertaining is done in restaurants or public venues, and very seldom is anyone invited into the home as these students were. Absolutely, positively, they were told, you must without exception eat whatever you are served. To show any hesitation about the food would be a terrific affront—it would destroy their testimony.

We both love Latin American cuisine of all kinds, but tamales for breakfast is a bit much for either of us. Nevertheless, that's what Melanie endured for the cause of Christ one morning. Her stomach had cause for complaint, but not her hosts.

We Americans have such a variety of low-cost food that we can indulge the luxury of pickiness. Obviously, this is an unwise habit for a young man going into the world. Hal admits to being a meat-and-potatoes man with a limited affection toward vegetables but decided to try and avoid developing that in his sons. At early ages, as we introduced new foods, we would offer them to the youngsters as something really great.

"What's that?" the four-year-old would ask.

"Black olives!" exclaimed Hal, who really doesn't care for them. "Do you want one?"

Curious, the little guy would try them, and after a moment, decide that black olives were the best thing he had ever encountered. Marketing is important, you see.

This kind of strategy hasn't made Hal much friendlier toward vegetables, but it's created a bunch of boys who will eat nearly anything. Managers of Indian restaurants are amazed to see young Americans digging into curry and daal and biryani. The boys nearly fight to see who gets the little octopus at the Chinese restaurants. When we visited Asia as a family, the boys took everything in stride. Fish served with the eyes? "Hey, do we eat those, too? Okay!"

We do allow each child one food item that they just can't bring themselves to eat. One of them has a horror of mayonnaise, for example; another wasn't fond of peanuts or peanut butter. They are still expected to be polite about their preferences, and they have to tolerate others enjoying that item without making an issue of it. They are also aware that if it comes to eating it or offending someone, they should be prepared to eat it.

If dinnertime behavior or complaining or general manners get too egregious, we make the offender stand up for a time — maybe sixty seconds — while the rest of us continue eating. That's hard time for a hungry male. If that doesn't work, they might be sent away from the table altogether, and only allowed to finish when everyone they've offended is done.

We also do some formal training at home, making holiday meals a time to bring out the silver and china. We organize formal parties around Christmas and New Year's Day, just for our extended family and occasionally a few friends. At our annual Christmas Eve party, we lay out a spread of Christmas sweets and savories: cookies, fruitcake, meatballs, meat and cheese trays, crackers and dip, cheese balls, hot tea, all sorts of party foods. We use formal dishes and table decorations - the very best we have, even if only our family will be there. We serve ourselves and talk and visit, later singing carols and reading the Christmas story. This is one of our children's favorite events and people in our area love to be invited. We want to build happy memories and let our children see that we consider our family worth the best we have to offer. However, the experience of handling a plate through a buffet line and neatly eating fancy finger foods and hors d'oeuvres gives the boys confidence when we take them to a formal event or reception outside the home.

Finally, we have to remember that a meal is a time of fellowship, not just a refueling stop. Hal often remarked that meals with business colleagues could be stressful because of their tendency to bolt their food; some seemed unused to conversation at the table, though not in a particular hurry to leave once done. We make a point to talk together at dinner, keeping an eye on the manners of course — not an easy task with eight children gathered around — to help them develop the ability to pace a conversation around the admitted purpose of eating, too.

Deportment

Will proper manners feminize our boys, lessening their masculinity to some extent? Of course not. It is true, though, that etiquette can be observed in a manly fashion, or it can be dainty and over-nice. Proper grammar doesn't require an affected tone or exaggerated enunciation, and gracious behavior can be a confident expression of strength with self-control. Some of our country's greatest leaders were well-trained in social graces; George Washington, Robert E. Lee, and Theodore Roosevelt were known for their faultless manners, yet they held the loyalty of rough-necked men who were willing to die on their orders.

Fathers need to keep an eye on their sons' posture and nonverbal communication; the boys at the park didn't know that men don't sit that way, and their mother didn't realize their feminine mannerisms could be sending a dangerous and ambiguous signal to observers. Mama will teach them not to slouch, but it may take Dad to show them how to square their shoulders and walk purposefully.

Fathers need to teach their sons how to stand tall and project a masculine confidence even — especially — in uncertain situations. Some boys will need more coaching than others. Smaller boys — and be aware that some are small in spirit though not in body — may need role models for this. "Son, pretend you're Samson. How would Samson walk? How would he stand?" Does Samson walk with his head down, avoiding eye contact? Or does he walk with head held high, unafraid? When he crosses his arms, does it look like he's hugging himself for comfort? Does he swing his arms at his side, or does he flutter his hands close to his chest?

Help your son present himself in a manner other boys will respect. Teaching your son to carry himself with confidence can help avoid confrontations with those playground bantams looking for a smaller chicken to peck. It's important to remember, too, that this is time for training the men of the future, not holding young boys to a standard you'd expect of a young adult. An occasional gesture or mannerism that might be more appropriate from their sisters needs coaching, not disciplinary action — at young ages in particular, how are they to know?

There are other issues of manners which are peculiar to men. We teach our sons there is a sort of *noblesse oblige* in their strength; a man should use his muscular strength to help those around him. Hal tells the boys their mother should never have to carry anything unless everyone else's arms are full, first. We encourage them to look for opportunities to use their strength for others — holding the door for ladies or people with burdens, giving a hand to a younger sibling by lifting something or bringing it down to them, looking for jobs to do at their grandmothers' homes, or offering to help women unloading their carts at the grocery store.

Likewise they know to give up their seats to their elders and especially to ladies. We tell them that when an adult enters the room, if no other seats are available the boy should casually stand or move to the floor. The goal is to be polite, not ostentatious.

Striking a balance in cleanliness is another area that must be addressed. Too often, mothers hate to see their sons get dirty and fuss at them for it. It is important that men not be afraid to get and be dirty. Where would our world be if the Allied forces had been unable to stand trench life in World War I? Many things men must do require them to get sweaty and covered in grime. We do our sons no favor to make them shrink from those tasks. On the other hand, it is the peak of discourtesy to care so little about your hygiene and appearance that you nauseate those around you. Seems obvious, but we have found it is not at all obvious to boys. Have you ever had this conversation?

> Mom [disgusted]: "Son, go take a shower."
> Son [puzzled]: "Why, Mom?"
> Mom [at her limit]: "You stink!"
> Son [cheerful]: "That's all right. I don't mind!"
> Mom: [loses it]

Boys need to be taught that it is completely unacceptable to go out in public, to a non-dirty situation of any kind, unless you are clean and appropriately dressed. Seriously, boys often don't smell themselves or realize they have greasy hair. Those things have to be taught. They have to be taught that deodorant is non-optional. Guys will frequently buck you on this because they see it as something only women care about. This is the only real downside we see to leaving the dating culture behind: teenagers trying to find a date will clean up their act in high school, while our boys who are trying hard *not* to pay attention to girls seem to lack motivation to keep themselves clean.

You've got to draw a serious line in the sand here or they will embarrass you - and themselves - again and again. We found to our dismay that our very manly son whom we had intentionally raised to take dirt and sweat in stride was pretty clueless about the social effects of stinking. He moved in a circle too polite to call him on it (less polite friends may have helpfully observed, "Man, you *reek*"), so we had to be the heavies. You have got to raise boys that know when to get filthy and when to clean up. It's all about appropriateness.

Appropriateness in dress is a frustration for boys sometimes, too. One son is comfortable only in T-shirts and shorts. Another always wants to be dressed for success and wouldn't wear shorts even at the *beach* if we didn't insist. Our guys need to know how to dress up and how to dress down.

A college admissions officer told us that he can tell when a young man he is interviewing is wearing dress clothes for the first time. The unfamiliar clothing (*What do I do with this tie?*) makes the fellow uneasy and it negatively affects how he presents himself. Our goal is to raise men that are comfortable in any situation in which God places them. To do that, they've got to be comfortable dressed up. Nearly all men will have to dress up for some critical things in their lives: job interviews, weddings and funerals, at a minimum. At occasions that are already so stressful, their discomfort in their clothing shouldn't be adding to it.

We recommend that every boy have at least a nice pair of khakis, a solid color buttondown shirt and a tie and that he be made to wear them when appropriate enough that he's comfortable in them. By the time a son is 16 or so, he really needs to add a jacket to that. If you can only afford one, we recommend a blazer over a suit - it is more versatile and it is easier to change out the pants as he grows before the coat needs a new size. He should be trained to notice how others are dressed and how he can alter his outfit to suit the occasion. If things are a little more casual than expected, he can take off his tie or jacket. If they're a lot more casual, he can take off both and even roll up his sleeves. As Christians, we should strive to make sure our appearance is not a distraction from our message. That means we shouldn't draw attention to ourselves by being either over- or under-dressed. The son that is only comfortable in long pants, a button-down and a nice belt — we had one of those — needs to be taught those are inappropriate at the gym or while framing a house. It ruins his more expensive good clothes, which is discourteous to his family, and it gives a wrong impression of being a little too nice to the boys around him. You've got to teach them balance.

Their strength and energy are also challenges they need to control. Frankly, we must constantly remind our growing sons that indoors is just not the place for roughhousing; the furniture may survive boisterous behavior when the boys are six and four, but ten years later the same thing creates scrap lumber. They have to recognize their mass and power are destructive forces in the homes of older folk, in stores and public places.

Parents of boys do learn to tolerate, or at least to expect, a certain level of noise at home. They have a tendency to walk like young elephants, and it may be difficult to explain the problem to them. Hal remembers being a teenager and totally confused when his parents asked him to *walk* more quietly. It wasn't until he had to learn a smoother stride in marching band that he realized it was possible to walk without slamming his heels down every step. You don't want to create sons with a mincing step; maybe the best illustration to use is a commando or wilderness scout, who has to cover territory — no time for tip-toe — without crashing through the underbrush and alerting the enemy or prey.

They will need help learning their "indoor voice" as well. We frequently remind them at the dinner table, "We're all right here; you don't have to shout." This is a good time to teach them parliamentary procedure, or in other words, that one person has the floor at a time. It's important that they know their home is a place that appreciates their masculinity, but they also have to respect the needs of gentleness and some quietude for their mother in the home they share. The most essential point is that we teach them to act appropriately inside or out, at home or in public.

Social Interaction

We were raised in the South and taught from the earliest ages to say "Yes, sir" and "No, ma'am" to anyone older or in authority. Parents of friends were "Mr. Young" or "Mrs. Young;" only the very closest family intimates were promoted to "Uncle Hal" or "Aunt Melanie," although these are common in other cultures.

The accepted terms of respect vary around the country; we've lived places where polite children were expected to call us "Brother Hal" and "Sister Melanie," or "Mr. Hal" and "Miss Melanie" (regardless of marital status). The critical issue is to show people the respect they expect. It was a difficult adjustment, after such an upbringing and four years in the military, for Hal to call supervisors and managers "Bob" or "Jim", but that was their request and expectation. It would have been impolite, in fact, *disrespectful*, to do otherwise. Paul said, *"I have become all things to all men, that I might by all means save some."* [8]

Teach your sons to study carefully what the prevailing standard appears to be, and to adjust their address to keep in step with the best expectations of the present culture.

Out of the Greenhouse

Our state homeschool organization adopted the motif of a greenhouse for the process of home education. The sheltered environment allows the gardener to give young plants an early start under the best possible conditions, even if the outside is still inclement. At the proper time, those plants will be "hardened off", preparing them for a transition to the outdoors.

So it is with our sons. When they first start to show early signs of maturity and self-control, which we expect around 13 or 14 years old, we begin taking them to adult functions whenever we can. While it raises eyebrows occasionally, we've found many meetings will accept a well-behaved, well-dressed young man who sits quietly outside the circle of adults and just listens. We've taken the boys to meetings of political parties and non-profit boards, conferences and seminars, receptions and other events. We'll brief the boys beforehand, emphasize they are guests and not participants, and discuss the event thoroughly afterward. Recently Hal took our 16-year-old son Caleb with him to a two-day seminar on investigative journalism techniques. When Hal was president of the state homeschool association, John Calvin was his aide-de-camp; our eldest son became so familiar in state political circles that leaders often looked past Hal and asked, "Where's John?", when he entered the room.

By the time they graduate from high school, they have been given a chance to be introduced to leaders in the community, to look in on the world of grown up affairs, and to gain familiarity with situations they will soon encounter as adults in their own right. And the benefit is mutual — when leaders get to know our sons as polite and thoughtful young adults, it has opened doors for internships and volunteer positions, opportunities to write for publication, requests to help with church ministries, job offers and more.

Conclusion

Manners, really, are a matter of consideration toward others and humility toward ourselves, with the hope that our courtesy will keep us from causing offense to our neighbor or damage to our testimony. It is not a feminine affectation, but a challenge to young men to be like the ideal knights — fierce in battle, but refined in society. A young man who respects himself as a man and shows it in his carriage, who knows how to treat others even in unfamiliar circumstances, can be comfortable and confident wherever God places him.

NOTES FOR CHAPTER 11

[1] In Mandarin, the phrase "to give a clock" sounds similar to phrases about funerals and cemeteries or so we're told. The face-saving response is for the recipient to hand the giver a token piece of money, to make the gift into a "purchase."

[2] 1 Peter 3:8

[3] Romans 12:10, 16

[4] James 1:19

[5] Romans 12:16; Proverbs 18:13

[6] Titus 3:2

[7] Leviticus 19:14; Proverbs 26:18-19; Ephesians 5:4

[8] 1 Corinthians 9:22

12

KP Isn't Women's Work

We love history. Naturally, we've enjoyed taking the children to visit living history exhibitions like Colonial Williamsburg and Jamestown Settlement in Virginia. One thing is always very evident—the men will demonstrate manly arts like blacksmithing, carpentry, coopering and printing, while the women are busy in the kitchen or the laundry, or making soap and candles, or spinning and weaving and sewing the clothes. There may be some crossover taking care of the small animals and fowl in the barnyard, but gender roles are pretty clearly delineated elsewhere.

The reason for the separation is pretty obvious when you consider the brute strength required for many jobs in the 17th century. Men are built for more rugged use, and it is hard to imagine a colonial lady stoking up the forge and shoeing a Clydesdale—not that wash day was a picnic in 1620, either, but it's a matter of degree.

Have times changed? Well, certainly, but does that change our criteria for "appropriate" work for sons compared to daughters, for husbands compared to wives?

Several years ago a friend was talking with Melanie about their philosophies of raising boys. The friend said she made sure her sons did *men's* work—outside jobs, cleaning the garage, and so forth—never the *women's* work. At the time, we had six boys and no girls at all. Melanie staggered mentally at the thought of washing laundry for six boys and husband, and picking up after the whole crew, totally by herself, while Hal and the boys divided responsibility for a third-acre yard. Still, it's helpful to examine preconceptions from time to time, and the friend had unknowingly raised the question—were we harming our sons' self-perception and manliness by expecting them to share in the household duties too?

We had come at the question a bit differently than our friends. We both agreed that the husband was the leader of the family and the primary financial support, while the wife was meant to be the household manager and keeper of the home.[1] We were best friends before we considered marriage, though, so as newlyweds we just liked being together (we still do). We found it was enjoyable to work together outside, then come in and do the indoor tasks together, all the time carrying on an intense political or philosophical discussion. It was better than working apart all day.

Melanie's parents had much the same experience—they were friends from childhood and hated to be apart. For most of her childhood, Melanie's family owned a retail business, and since Daddy and Mama worked together there, they pretty much raised the children at the store too—it's where Melanie and her brother played and ate and studied. She remembers Daddy didn't do housework, but he provided Mama with hired help since she was with him instead of at home all day.

Hal's parents took their own approach as well. His father liked to experiment in the kitchen, and enjoyed trying ethnic foods and creating new recipes. His mom enjoyed painting and remodeling projects in the house. Maybe both of us had a little non-traditional home life, compared to friends whose parents followed very rigid gender expectations around the house.

We need to be careful of thinking or saying that a decision is probably right because that's the way it's always been, or that's the way we were raised, or the way our parents did it. We're called to live lives that are holy, set apart from the world's expectations, so we have to question things more than our neighbor. So forgetting our newlywed experience or our parents' examples, were we wrong to require young men to do dishes and laundry? Are they forced out of God's design by pushing a mop around the kitchen floor?

A Biblical look at work roles

Think back over the typical "women's roles" from the historic exhibits, then compare to the Biblical record; they don't correspond exactly. Textile work is frequently singled out for women, yet God specially commissioned two *men*, Bezelel the son of Uri and Aholiab the son of Ahisamach, to design, teach, and do the work of weaving, engraving, and making embroidered tapestry and fine linen for the tabernacle; they also sewed the priests' garments.[2] Paul and Aquila both sewed tents by profession.[3] There are numerous *commandments* for men to wash their own clothing, and the Greek word for launderer is a masculine noun.[4]

Cooking is another "womanly" task, yet Hosea 7:4 describes men as bakers. Abraham's cook was a young man, and Isaac instructed his son to cook dinner before receiving his blessing.[5] The Levites cooked for their brethren in the Temple service so their duties could proceed uninterrupted.[6] The disciples *did as Jesus had directed them; and they prepared the Passover.*[7]

Even caring for the baby is fair game for Dad. Moses complained to God, *"Have I begotten this people, that thou shouldst say unto me, 'Carry them in thy bosom, as a nursing father beareth the suckling child ... '"* The Lord uses the same term, speaking through

Isaiah of the restoration of Israel, saying, *"Behold, I will lift up mine hand to the Gentiles ... and they shall bring thy sons on their arms and thy daughters upon their shoulders, and kings shall be thy nursing fathers ... "*[8] When Hal was in the military, some thought it harmed the image of officers to be seen carrying babies; obviously that wasn't based on Scripture.

Even In Our Culture

There are plenty of examples within our own culture; in fact, the military provides prime examples. The thought of a young man stirring a pot being less than manly doesn't stand up to KP duty in the military; "Cookie" serving in the chow line is almost always portrayed as a sweating bruiser of a man. Sailors were called "swabbies" because mopping the deck was their daily task. Does it make a difference that the sailor wore white bell–bottoms and a square collar? Maybe if we provide our sons with a business–like canvas apron rather than one of Mom's, we could see kitchen duty in a different light at home, too.

In civilian life too, men are tailors and dry cleaners, and the most famous chefs are men. So why would we balk at asking our sons to do similar tasks for the family?

Could it be that we place a different valuation on work that's done for pay, as a career, for somebody outside the home? That is something worth examining, too. Do we consciously or unconsciously hold a greater respect for the woman who teaches fourth grade at the local elementary school than we do for the woman teaching *three* grade levels to her children at home? Why? Is there less burden of planning and instruction for Mom to teach multiple sections of each subject every day? Granted, there are differences in the two tasks, but the point is that the basic task of *teaching* is the same.

Likewise, when something that is considered woman's work in the home is a perfectly acceptable way for a man to go out into the world and provide a living, where's the distinction? Was it doing it at home that was the problem for our friend? Perhaps so. In most families in our circle, the father works outside the home and the mother does not. Since the home is her main sphere of influence and her husband is gone from home for many hours a day, she takes the chief burden in doing the tasks of the home. Because of this, the household tasks within the home are thought of as women's work.

Melanie says that she was surprised to find that Hal didn't share her friend's position on "appropriate" work for her sons; in fact, he's the one who brought up the military examples. She admits she wishes she had talked to him sooner rather than later! Whether boys should do housework had never come up before.

Mission Critical Tasks

One of the more memorable briefings Hal received in the military was at summer training in ROTC. A clergyman introduced himself to the cadets with the statement, "The mission of the Chaplain Corps is 'Bombs On the Target'."

Certainly that was an arresting kind of remark to hear from a minister of the gospel. His point though was that every job in the Air Force was meant to support the larger purpose, that of defending the United States' people by projecting military power in support of national policy. Since the spiritual needs of military personnel are real and in some ways more pronounced than in the general populace, it was important that the military have chaplains to address those needs so they didn't become a hindrance to mission.

When David and his men rescued their families and belongings from the Amalekites, he vetoed the suggestion that only those in the fight should have a part in the rewards; *"As his part is who goes down to the battle,* so shall *his part* be *who stays by the supplies; they shall share alike,"* he ordered.[9] Those whose service was in the rear were still part of the army. Likewise, we need to help our sons see that any service that advances the family's mission is worthwhile and needs to be valued. Where would the family be if no one cooked, washed, cleaned, or took care of the myriad other things around the household?

By our decision to reclaim the educational process and teach our children at home, we put Melanie in the position where she does not have the time to do the majority of the housework on her own. Our financial situation made a hired housekeeper just a dream, so as the family grew and the housework expanded, it was plain our sons needed to be brought into action to keep the ship of our home afloat. When there are no big sisters to be mother's apprentices, there's not much to debate about.

We do make an effort to make the indoor chores a little more boy-friendly. The young man assigned as cook for the day is "The Chef." Jobs are spoken of in terms of jurisdictions[10] or duties — "Who is in charge of the den?" — to emphasize that they have responsibility and authority to contribute to the family through household chores. We try to emphasize that the appliances are performing work that we would have to do ourselves — a task brought into high relief when the dishwasher broke down and a part had to be ordered! Hal is known to chide the laundryman of the day, "Your servants are waiting for instructions," when he notices the washer and dryer standing idle.

Young men are capable of complex tasks if they're properly trained *and supervised.* Young boys can help with straightening and sweeping, putting away laundry, and washing cabinets and baseboards. We start seven- or eight-year-olds with laundry, holding the entire family responsible to keep lights, darks, and reds separate (admittedly, a constant battle). The same age can tackle bathrooms and more substantial cleaning tasks like windows.

Even a nine-year-old can prepare simple meals, even for a large family, and some of ours have gotten very good at it. We've noticed a need for ongoing advice in this area — some become a bit adventurous experimenting with ingredients, while others tend to invent shortcuts. All of them have needed help learning to plan ahead a few steps and carry out cooking tasks in parallel, so everything gets to the table reasonably hot and dinner doesn't take two hours to prepare. You can explain this in terms of project management skills — a very important task for adult work.

"Presentation" usually doesn't come naturally, either; you have to decide for your family whether a sandwich on a paper towel is acceptable, or if it calls for a plate (just handing them out like you're dealing cards doesn't pass here).

In all of these things, you the parent can make the job more suitable for your sons, either by being alert to get tools and supplies they're comfortable with — some of ours suffer from very dry skin, so gloves are a help bordering on necessity — or by simplifying some tasks, like browning hamburger in bulk and freezing it in small portions for use in spaghetti or chili. In fact, the boys love bulk cooking. The huge quantities and enormous pots are interesting in themselves, but they really love working together in an assembly line. The industrialization of cooking appeals to the engineer in them, and it speeds up the daily task *immensely*. Take advantage of this!

When it comes to boys and household tasks, we really don't need to worry if they will be harmed by doing "women's work". Scripture doesn't make many distinctions, and if we go about it the right way, there's no cultural reason they can't help around the house, either. The important things to keep in mind are twofold — our sons need to learn these tasks to take care of themselves when they leave our homes, and they need to understand them as a crucial part of the family's mission *now*. KP is not women's work in the Army, and it isn't around our house, either.

Notes for Chapter 12

[1] Titus 2:5. Interestingly, when Paul said women were to be "keepers at home" (KJV), he used a term which implies more than just housework. A similar term is used for a gardener. It implies someone who is more than just a worker, but a watcher and overseer or manager of the thing as well.

[2] Exodus 35:30–35; 39:1 (see also 38:22–23)

[3] Acts 18:2–3

[4] Numbers 8:21 refers to the purification of the Levites for service in the Tabernacle; they were all adult men. There are dozens of references to a man washing his clothing for ritual impurity. Mark 9:3 is the only use of the term *gnafeus* for a fuller (KJV) or launderer (NKJV), but it appears in the Greek Old Testament (the Septuagent) in 2 Kings 18:17 and Isaiah 7:3 and 36:2.

[5] Genesis 18:7, 27:4.

[6] 2 Chronicles 35:14–15

[7] Matthew 26:19

[8] Numbers 11:12, Isaiah 49:22–23 (KJV). Newer translations render the term "guardian" or "foster father", which basically means the same thing; a foster mother of an infant would be expected to nurse the child, after all.

[9] 1 Samuel 30:24

[10] We first heard them called jurisdictions by the Duggar family.

13

LOVE AND WAR

Recently we were gathered with several families at our weekly Bible study, where we are reading through the Bible in sequence. Usually, we take turns reading the passage, each person reading a verse or two or three. This evening we had reached Ezekiel 23, so we opened up the scheduled passage and took off reading. By the second reader, voices were already getting strained and faces flushed. The passage very graphically describes the harlotry of Israel. It was driven home to us that sexual sin is nothing new in this world - and our children were going to be exposed to it.

The federal Department of Education has a section called the National Center for Educational Statistics. NCES collects and analyzes data on all kinds of issues of education, from preschool through university levels. In the past ten years, it has begun publishing findings on homeschooling, mainly collected through a random survey process that encompasses all types of educational arrangements.

One of the most basic questions to researchers is why parents choose to educate their children at home. Studies and surveys since the late 1970s reliably found two reasons at the top, close enough they took turns being number one: a desire to give children an education in line with the parents' religious beliefs, and a dissatisfaction with the quality of institutional education generally. This is why some researchers have divided the homeschooling movement into "ideologues," who want to teach a certain philosophy, and "pedagogues," who want to use a particular teaching style.

In 2003, NCES reported a different result. Although religious or academic reasons were in the top three, as always, the sample of that year's study ranked "concern about the environment of other schools" higher than either one. Instead of protesting the content or methods of the schools, parents were rejecting the social aspect of institutional school, the peer group which the schools provided.[1]

"Right. What *about* socialization?" replied the veteran homeschoolers.

A friend of ours was a school resource officer in a small Southern town. After serving in this role for several years, he requested a transfer assignment from the large high school he patrolled to one of the smaller rural schools out in the county. He told us privately that he was simply fed up with the school's tolerance for sexual activity on campus; at least, that was his perception, as he had been told not to interfere with students trysting in various combinations of male and female around the school grounds. Like Lot, his soul was vexed by what he was forced to endure. As long as there was no threat of bloodshed, use of controlled substances, or illegal parking, the *policeman* was told to just move along.

The bar of acceptable behavior continues to lower, and as we continue sinking in our post-Christian ethics, the amount of sexual temptation presented to our children is only going to increase. Unfortunately, if we don't recognize how much temptation is already burdening our children, we may take a false hope in simply withdrawing them from bad company. What they need is help dealing with the temptation they carry within.

Time to talk, and not to the kids

This is plainly an area where parents aren't talking with one another. Mothers we've met, particularly homeschooling mothers, seem to be in denial about their children's sexuality. It's as if the kids never quite leave the baby stage — you know, when you dress the little girls in pink and the little boys in blue because, frankly, they still look identical any place but the bath tub. Moms worry that talking to their children about sex will destroy their innocence and expose them to a Pandora's box of temptations.

Fathers know better, if they're honest about it. They know that temptation is an ongoing battle for nearly every man, and it starts much earlier than most women realize. Boys don't need exposure to *anything* to find sexual temptation; all the pleasure points are easily accessible, and they discover that fact before they can talk about it. Parents will correct outward behavior that might be embarrassing ("Get your finger out of your nose! Keep your hands out of your pants") but without some broader principle of why and how to avoid that temptation, curiosity will hatch into fascination and progress to real problems later on. Peeking at risque magazines when they're ten years old is *way* down the road from the starting point.

Simply put, our sons are sinners. They inherit it from us, but they quickly add up their own records on top of the original sin. In this area, shielding is not enough — not even if we kill the TV and ban movies and heavily censor our books and protect the children from immoral companions and never talk to them about sex. It's not enough.

Of course, a lot of that kind of vigilance will be needed, too. We don't watch broadcast or cable television at home for a variety of reasons, but our children are still exposed to it at their grandparents' and friends' homes. We do still watch some TV occasionally ourselves, like when we're traveling and staying in hotels. Recently we were relaxing after a homeschool conference and tuned in a really good special on The History Channel; it was Memorial Day weekend and they were talking about D-Day and afterward. We had to stay on top of the remote, though, because nearly every station break had been purchased by a manufacturer with a new sexual product and a very graphic commercial to introduce it. If Hal hadn't seen the ad on a business trip earlier, no one would have known what was coming, and the first viewing could have planted the image forever.

Another time we were visiting family and Hal took the children out so Melanie could rest for the afternoon. Melanie was expecting, and when she saw an advertisement for an upcoming program about babies on one of the health channels, she decided to watch. Imagine her surprise when the program opens with video of a couple in the act, their faces blurred but the private parts made very, very public. This was mid-afternoon programming on a regular cable channel.

Evidently if you use medical terminology it's not pornographic. Well, *that's* helpful to know.

If children in a Christian, homeschooling, conservative, seldom-TV-watching family could be accidentally exposed to that, is any child safe? If your child never goes through the checkout line, if you refuse to visit a home which owns a television set, if your town forbids outdoor advertising and animals in your neighborhood never breed, your child *still* isn't protected enough. You might as well say you never read Scripture, either; one young man confessed to us that he was struggling with sexual temptation largely because he had read an Old Testament passage that warned against it.[2]

If the power of sin is so perverse and our hearts so prone to follow it, then our sons (and we ourselves) need two things: we need to know how to resist temptation and repent when we fall, and we need to have a changed heart that gives us the will to do it.

Talk is not cheap, it's essential

The cavalry commander Nathan Bedford Forrest is said to have summarized his basic strategy of mobility and massed forces: "Get there firstest with the mostest." That's a good strategy for teaching your sons in this area — be the first one to give him a context for understanding sex.

We know that God created the marriage relationship and that *Marriage is honorable among all, and the bed undefiled.*[3] The term for bed in the original Greek is *koite,* the source of the term "coitus;" it's not talking about sleep here. Sex within marriage is a gift of God, and the world continues to try and separate the two. Ideally, long before our sons are hit by surging hormones, they will know that God created sex, and He blesses it when we follow His rules about it. They'll know the facts about reproduction with a godly perspective, and they won't feel a need to ferret out information they couldn't find at home, finding it from sources that don't have their interests at heart. We may find it embarrassing to discuss the topic with our children but the world and the devil have no qualms at all.

Often the uneasiness we feel about a situation is rooted in its unfamiliarity. If we don't know where to start, the first step will look like a doozy. If we can make the discussion as natural as possible, it will take a lot of the mystery out of the whole subject; it could be a reasonable Q&A subject between parent and child, no different than questions about math or history.

Start by being alert to the teachable moment; even this subject has one. When your young son begins to play with himself in the bathtub, don't freak out — take the chance to explain, "Son, I know it feels good to touch yourself there, but those feelings are something God wants you to save until you're married. In fact, if you keep on doing it, you'll be sinning. You don't want to sin against God, do you? Well, I don't want you to either, so just wash yourself down there and move on. It'll wait until you have a wife."

C. S. Lewis in his book *Miracles* says that it is hard for us to appreciate something which is radically different than our experience. As earthbound creatures for this time, it is hard for us to grasp the full wonder of heaven. Lewis compares it to attempting to explain to a boy that sex is better than chocolate. Since the boy only connects with the idea of chocolate, the subtle and the sublime aspects of marital union kind of blow past him.

We have to remember this when we talk with our children about sex. It is easy to get clinical (the infamous "plumbing lecture") or wax eloquent about the spiritual nature of it, either way trying to hide our embarrassment behind a veil of language. What we have to keep in mind is the boy doesn't get the two-become-one-flesh mystery; he just knows he's curious, and certain things tantalize him. As someone said, you have to put the hay where the horse can get it.

Melanie found an effective approach using the concept of a long-anticipated present at Christmas or birthday times — a child has to be pretty unusual not to have a very definite idea what *that's* all about. The parable goes like this:

> *The special feelings and the physical relationship of married people are like a gift put out long before the holiday. You might be tempted to open it and play with it, but if you do that, trouble is coming. You might think you'll*

just shake it and try to figure out what's inside, but when you're shaking it, you find a corner of the paper is up—and you think maybe you'll just carefully take the paper off—just to take a look. And once it's uncovered you realize you've got a really wonderful gift here! There are so many pieces! It looks like such fun! Surely there's no reason not to play with it now, since it will be yours soon ... but you keep jumping up to hide it, though, because you think you hear somebody coming and you'll be in trouble. It turns out that's not as much fun as you hoped, and when you decide to put it back together, some of the pieces are missing and the paper's torn. When the big day comes, your "wonderful gift" is damaged, and you have to confess what you've done and feel shame and embarrassment. It is never the same again, and you can't undo what you've done.

God's gift of sex is very much like that. If you try to use it too soon, before you are married, you not only sin against the One who gave you the gift, God, but in many ways you ruin the gift for yourself and also for the person you will love the most on earth, your wife. Because you see, it's her gift, too.

At the moment, our state is in the midst of a controversy about sex education in the schools. For almost fifteen years, the public school policy has been to teach abstinence only; this year, the legislature is about to enact a change in favor of comprehensive sex ed.

We have our own sort of "comprehensive" program, though it's not about how to avoid AIDS or obtain family planning services. We try to give our sons the total Biblical context about sex—the way God intends it to be used, both for celebrating the total union between husband and wife, and for the conception of children. The world desperately wants to separate the sexual act from the intended results (not "consequences"). God pushes them firmly together.

This means talking about sexual temptation can very easily lead into discussions about pregnancy, labor, childbirth, and breastfeeding. One little boy we knew very sheepishly asked his pregnant mother what machine the doctor would use to get the baby out of her. She gently explained that her body would push the baby out.

"But how?" he asked. "How will the baby come out?" A very reasonable question, you know.

She explained that there was a secret passage the baby would use.

"Can I see it?" Another reasonable question for a five-year-old boy.

"No, son," she explained. "There are parts of our bodies that God wants us to keep covered except within our marriage, or if we need help from a doctor."

He was happy and satisfied with that explanation. It was age appropriate, it showed him that his parents would respect his questions, and ended when he'd heard enough.

It's like the first grader who asked, "Where did I come from?" After a tense explanation of the birds and bees, his mom takes a breath and asks, "Does that make sense?"

"I think so," he said, still puzzled. "But Jimmy is from Cleveland, and now I don't know what to tell him."

Sometimes difficult conversations are easier in a particular venue. We've had some useful talks riding in the car; parent and son are both facing forward and not at each other! This works even better at night. Like so many other things, finding — or prompting — a teachable moment makes a big difference.

The Battlefield of the Mind

One of the most strenuous battles young men face is keeping their thought life pure. If you step back objectively and try to see things from the perspective of a visitor — say, what if you were an angel — it is incredible how saturated our culture is with sexual messages. It's so prevalent that we adults, particularly those who have a rightful outlet for our sexual desires, can become blasé about the sensuality of advertising and entertainment.

We need to help equip our sons to keep their thoughts away from sexual sin, and that will mean training them to keep their eyes away from the imagery that surrounds them. Job the righteous said, "*I have made a covenant with my eyes; how can I look on a maiden?*"[4] Fathers will need to be diligent to do the same; if Dad is ogling the young woman sunning herself on the beach, how can his teenaged son (who at least still has the moral right to marry her!) be expected to discreetly watch for shrimp boats on the horizon instead?

We need to teach them, though, the difference between temptation and sin. We tell them they can't help it if bird droppings land on their head, but if they reach up and massage it in, or sit hopefully under the nest waiting for something to fall, that's a different matter altogether.

Don't be afraid to ask your sons about their thought life, and frequently. Our church has a men's Bible study early on Monday mornings, and part of the routine is holding one another account-able for this; they actually ask one another if they've been looking at sensual images online or elsewhere. Just knowing that they will have to confess the sin or else lie about it is a helpful deter-rent. Likewise, we frequently ask our sons about their thought lives, not prying for details but simply to ask if they are having difficulties which we can help with.

Avoiding a Big Trap

The Internet is a special temptation to boys due to their sen-sitivity to visual inputs, the perceived privacy of online ex-periences, and the sheer availability of bad stuff out there. One doesn't have to go slumming in the pornographic neighborhoods to have difficulties; even the sidebar ads on news sites may have inappropriate dress or subject matter. Popular magazines at the library have advertisements with web addresses that lead to pornographic sites. Websites that are not problematic in and of themselves may have links to URLs that are risque or porno-graphic in content. Google searches on innocuous subjects may turn up sites that are downright shocking. Some pornographers have even purchased domain names similar to common home-work destinations and set out their traps; one famous example substituted ".com" for ".gov" on the end of the address used for a federal government website. Once hooked by the content, it is an easy matter for a boy to steal a few minutes while parents are busy cooking, caring for young siblings, or getting children ready for bed.

There are a number of different approaches to dealing with this threat. The most drastic is to eliminate Internet access al-together. Another is to subscribe to a service which only allows access to sites which the service has reviewed and placed on a "white list" of acceptable content. There are numerous software packages which try and block sites containing certain words or images.

Due to the nature of our family's work and ministries, we've needed more open access than that. Melanie, for example, provides lactation counseling for mothers with nursing problems; software which blocked every site containing the word "breast" would interfere with that ministry (though it would certainly present little problem for Hal's engineering work!).

First, we put the main computer in the family room, facing out into the room, so no one has total privacy online. We also installed a program called *Covenant Eyes* that doesn't block anything, but keeps a detailed record of every site visited. Periodically the program emails that list to a designated accountability partner; Hal sends his to Melanie, for example. This is installed on every computer the boys can access, including Dad's laptop and their grandmother's computer. Just knowing that someone will see that list can be a helpful deterrent.

A Fist to Knock Away Temptation

We do our best to protect our sons from temptation, but we know it is impossible to avoid it entirely - our own hearts provide temptation! Sons need to know what to do when they face the desire to sin. We tell our sons to use five important tools to fight off immoral thoughts:

1. **Leave the situation.** This is so important. If you are in the bathroom, get dressed and get out. If you are in bed, get up. If you are at a friend's house, go home. Leave a situation that tempts you.

2. **Pray** and ask the Lord for forgiveness and help.

3. **Read your Bible.** The Word is a light to our feet and will guide us to do what is right.

4. **Sing praises or hymns to God.** Sometimes music can break through the coldness of our hearts.

5. **Go to your authority and ask for help.** Our sons have each done this more than once. They say, "Mom and Dad, I just keep having bad thoughts. Will you pray for me?"

We lift a finger for each of these as we remind them, then close all five into a fist and say, "Five ways that make a fist to knock away temptation." We remind our sons of this often, because it is important that they realize that they are not helpless before temptation, but that God always gives a way of escape.

Finding a wife

Avoiding temptation and dealing with slips and falls is the battle line for our young men. They have to learn how to say NO to the traps laid on every side for them. However, we also have to prepare them for the time when they will say YES. They need be prepared for their future as husbands, when the full expression of their sexuality will not only be a pleasure but a duty!

Homeschoolers have engaged in a long-running discussion about the best way to honor God in finding a mate. Some of the speakers and authors we've seen support all the world's traditions short of premarital sex; others advocate arranged marriages where the bride and groom first meet at the altar!

The Scriptures don't give a definitive pattern except the example of Christ and the church. Isaac and Rebecca had an arranged marriage, while their son Jacob had a prolonged courtship. Boaz and Ruth came together under the terms of Levirate marriage, the Jewish custom of the kinsman redeeming a brother's widow. Joseph and Mary were engaged in a betrothal so binding it would have required a divorce action to separate them.

The earthly stories we've heard run the gamut, too, with both happy and disappointing outcomes from a variety of approaches. How should we guide our sons in this phase of life?

We're still looking forward to the first marriage in our family, so we don't have personal experience as parents to draw upon. What we *can* rely on is the Bible.

First, it is clear that sexual immorality is sin, and indulging in lustful thoughts is sin as well. It's a basic rule but in our culture it has to be taught explicitly.

We've also taught our boys the Golden Rule applies here — we do to others as we would want them to do to us. Any young lady they meet is almost certainly going to be someone else's wife (since only one will ultimately be their own). How would they want someone to treat *their* future wife? They shouldn't do anything toward that young lady that they wouldn't want to hear about their bride's past. That really clarifies it for a young man!

The Bible teaches us not to defraud one another in relationships.[5] Fraud is the practice of persuading someone to believe you have promised a thing which in fact you are unable or unwilling to deliver. How about winning the heart and affections of someone that you are not seriously considering for marriage? Isn't this what happens in the usual teenage dating situation? We teach our sons that the Biblical pattern expects them to be able to support a wife before they go out seeking one, which means they won't be "going steady" as 14-year-olds. They have a responsibility to guard the hearts of the young ladies they know, and not entangle them in a romantic web which frankly means very different things to a girl than it does to a boy.

Our sons needed some coaching on this. We've been very open in our family about talking about feelings and thinking deeply about the issues of life, and some of that spills over into the boys' conversations with friends. Being homeschooled, they haven't been subjected to the peer pressure that places a high value on male aloofness, cynicism, and studied posturing for "cool." Their willingness to talk sets them apart from a lot of the boys, and the girls really respond to it — in some cases, you might say they fall for it.

One of our sons is passionate about ideas, and he'll talk eloquently about them with friends of either gender. One young lady thought she was receiving privileged attention from him, and it was starting to turn her head. Thankfully, her family has the same views we do, and her father politely asked Hal if something was going on between our son and his daughter. The answer was no, our son talks that way to *everybody*, but we'll sit down with him and make sure he understands. We realized this is what was happening:

> Boy says: "I am passionate about this idea and these
>   are my hopes."
> Girl thinks: "He must be passionate about me. See how
>   he's sharing his heart!"

We've had to sit down with our sons and explain that their manners may accidentally be interpreted as romantic interest, and if they're not courting yet, they need to turn down the intensity, at least as the girl perceives it. Talk with other girls, or with groups of friends. Spread the time and attention around. Share the wealth, so to speak.

Speaking of wealth, a barber once asked one of our middle-schoolers, "Do you have a girlfriend?" Our son answered with mild surprise, "No, I can't support a wife yet!" We've taught our boys that the Bible places responsibility on the man to support his family, and the Biblical counsel is, *Prepare your outside work, / Make it fit for yourself in the field; / And afterward build your house.*[6] Don't go building romantic attachments when marriage is still well out of the question.

The attraction between male and female, even at ages we might consider quite young, is meant to lead toward union, and if marriage is not part of the picture soon, it can easily lead into sin. Why carry a candle into a powder magazine?

We do need to recognize the proverb says to *prepare* the fields, not necessarily to *harvest* them. There are some parents who are taking the Scriptural admonition and imposing the expectation that a young man must be well-established in business and own a home of some kind, preferably debt-free, before he is allowed to court their daughter. Some young men are taking this idea on themselves and refusing to consider marriage until a lofty goal of financial success is attained.

We'd suggest that such goals are usually not achieved until later in adult life, and often because of the mutual support, encouragement, and accountability gained from a godly spouse. There's also the consideration that the blessings of children are mentioned in the context of *youth* — not as a discouragement from having children late in life, but a recognition that family life starts early. Also, Paul encouraged Timothy to stand boldly in his role as a church leader in spite of his relative youthfulness, while the qualifications for leadership include marriage, successful leadership of the family, and, if children are present, a level of faithfulness among the offspring.[7] To us, all these things point to an earlier rather than later start to family life—not at age twelve, by any means, but neither waiting until forty-two.

Finally, the Word of God teaches us to honor our parents and to regard the instruction of our fathers and mothers. We've taught our sons that they need to seek the advice and blessing of their parents as they choose the young women they want to win as their wives. Once they receive that, we would expect them to seek the blessing of the parents of the young lady. This could be a bit tricky if her parents are not believers or if their background is very different from ours, but we expect our sons to do what they should Biblically and understand that it won't look just the same in another's life. Josh Harris discusses his experiences in this situation, seeking the approval of parents who are not on the same page, in his book, *Boy Meets Girl.* Jonathan Lindvall's testimony is similar and both stories worked out just fine.

We take exception to those who would present a list of steps that every courtship must follow; it's just not mandated in Scripture. Each of the stories cited earlier illustrates a facet of God's love to His people—Isaac's faith in his father's direction, the patience of Jacob, the redeemer Boaz, the mercy and faith of Joseph. Even negative stories of human love in Scripture illustrate the longsuffering of God; think of Hosea.

Our courtship story

Actually, we practiced courtship ourselves, though we didn't know it at the time. We went to the same university as freshmen and met in the honors program there. We quickly became best friends and enjoyed one another's company, even more after Hal came to Christ during the spring term. There was an uncomfortable moment for Melanie, when her mother came to visit during the year; she met Hal, liked him, and told Melanie on the elevator, "That's the man you're going to marry."

"Mom, don't ruin this friendship!" she protested. "We are *friends!*" As if romance and friendship were separate and mutually exclusive categories.

The next year Melanie transferred to a different university, but we stayed in touch by phone and letter (okay, so we're dinosaurs). That summer, Melanie served with an inner city ministry in Philadelphia while Hal went to summer school overseas and then training camp with ROTC. He wrote that summer that he had noticed something strange going on in his thinking: whenever he went out with a girl on campus, he found himself thinking, "She's really cute, but she's not as smart as Melanie," or "She's really smart, but she's not as cute as Melanie," or "She's really smart and cute, but she doesn't love the Lord like Melanie." Hal had finally concluded that if every girl he met was being compared to what he'd found in Melanie, why not cut to the chase and seek the Lord's will concerning the two of us together?

Melanie panicked. When she left Hal's college, he was a new believer, and she had not had time to think of him as a young but growing Christian. Quandary! She invited him to come visit when his college had a football game against another school near hers, thinking she could talk him out of this notion. Well, she succeeded, except that seeing Hal now after a year and a half of growing in the Lord impressed her in a very different way. While she was talking Hal out of a deeper relationship, she found herself talked into it!

By the end of the year, we knew the issue was not going away, so we actively sought God's will — did He intend for us to marry each other? We began visiting each other's families, spending a lot of time on the road but seeing one another in a variety of situations. We spent time working on family projects and taking excursions together. We also spent a tremendous amount of time talking; our friends laughed at us, but we made long lists of every issue we could imagine in marriage then talked them through. How many children? When? Who would handle finances? Should the wife work? All the way down to who would take out the trash. (Hal's answer: See "Children, How many")

As we went through the lists, God knit our hearts together, and when Hal formally proposed, we had no doubts at all. We'd already talked through most of the major issues and many of the minor things *before* we got engaged, while we could still be honest about it and walk away freely. Naturally we've changed our minds about a lot of those issues since then, but we grew into our current views together, in unity.

We are convinced that the strength of our marriage is due in a large part to the solid foundation God led us to through courtship. We started out as friends and we are still friends. Because companionship, prayer, and consideration for one another came first, our romance was free from the turmoil of adjusting to the "real person" after marriage. That allowed us to be madly in love without worries, fears, or frustrations. We are praying the Lord will give each of our sons the same incredible gift He gave us, before we even knew to ask for it!

NOTES FOR CHAPTER 13

[1] "Parents' Reasons for Homeschooling", in Princiotta, D. and Bielick, S. (2006). *Homeschooling in the United States: 2003*, (NCES 2006-042) U.S. Department of Education. National Center for Education Statistics, Washington, D.C.: 2005. Available online at http://nces.ed.gov/Pubsearch/pubsinfo. asp?pubid=2006042. Accessed 6/26/2009.

[2] His name was not Paul, but the apostle had the same confession. See Romans 7:5-13.

[3] Hebrews 13:4

[4] Job 3:11

[5] 1 Thessalonians 4:1-8

[6] 1 Timothy 5:8; Proverbs 24:27

[7] Psalm 127:4; 1 Timothy 4:12; 1 Timothy 3:1-13

14

FIRING THE ARROW

For the past several years, Hal has had a sideline to his regular business — he's become a freelance journalist, writing book reviews and investigative stories for a conservative newspaper at a capital city think tank.

Our eldest son John has many of the same interests, and his senior year in high school Hal negotiated with the editor of the paper to take a movie review John had written on approval basis. If he liked it, he could have first bid on buying the article; if he didn't, no loss.

John's a movie buff with a good eye for theme and purpose, and an excellent writer to boot. With some coaching from Dad on how to edit and re-write for newspaper purposes, John's article got a warm response from the editor. John was a published (and paid!) writer just turning 18 years old.

The next assignment was a news story, a very different matter from a movie review. John, like his mother, is gregarious in groups but not on the phone, and this story required a number of calls to strangers in responsible positions. Worse, he was calling college admissions officers, the very class of people he had just been cultivating for his own educational plans. The fact that all applications were in and acceptances received didn't make it easier.

Hal and Melanie were ruthless. John had to be the man and make those calls; he was no longer John the supplicant prospect, but John the investigative journalist. It was time to step up to the plate. John made the calls all right, with his parents standing by and coaching him between calls on how to introduce himself, how to organize the questions and manage the interview, and how to follow up the call with his notes and correspondence.

It was a difficult task, but he managed it in the end and found the next one easier to do. Soon he was writing regularly. While his classwork demands keep him busy during college terms, he can earn good money and build his resume during holidays and the summer, working from home on his own schedule. Not bad for a college kid!

As our sons enter the real world, we need to do the same thing on many different fronts. As we've discussed earlier, boys need as much responsibility and independence as they can handle faithfully, and it needs to grow as their maturity does. If we prepare them over several years, the transition to adulthood is going to be much smoother and less contentious for all of us than a quick kick out of the nest at age 18. To make this happen, though, we will need to transition our relationship with our sons as they become their own men.

Scripture says *Honor your father and your mother* and it doesn't say to stop when you get to be 15 or 18 or 21.[1] On the other hand, it is *children* who are told to *obey your parents in the Lord, for this is right.*[2] Clearly there comes a time when strict obedience gives way to the independence of an adult, while maintaining honor and respect. This is an awkward bridge to cross and many families stumble over it, damaging relationships along the way. We have found it is best to get there gradually, incrementally.

Becoming a Man

B iblically, we don't see the extended period of childhood that we call adolescence, and we don't accept the idea that teenage years are naturally meant to be full of rebellion, argument, *Sturm und Drang.* We decided to give a different expectation to our sons: when they begin to reach the physical maturity of men, then we expect them to start acting like men.

Many cultures have some kind of coming-of-age ceremony. Maybe the closest thing in America now is high school graduation, though the legal thresholds of 18 and 21 are significant for some. We decided to adapt the ideas of friends who had created their own events to mark this transition. The Jewish tradition for boys is the Bar Mitzvah, "Son of the Law," observance; a Christian parallel might be a Bar Chanon, "Son of Grace," ceremony, as one of our friends called it.

The form we took for this is to have a party sometime around the boy's thirteenth birthday, inviting extended family and the families of men who have influence in our son's lives. We ask each man (and the grandmothers, since both our fathers have passed away) to bring a brief message or charge for our son to remember as he grasps his changing role in becoming a man. Often a gift symbolizing the message is included.

Our third son Matthew, for example, is the most organized member of the family; if you suddenly need a tool, chances are Matthew has one in his pocket or his briefcase. His grandmother gave him an antique carpenter's plane that had belonged to his grandfather; her challenge to him was to use his life's work to create things of beauty, precision, and usefulness, but to be cautious not to use his skills to deface or destroy the works around him. One of the fathers present gave him a small but powerful flashlight in recognition of his constant state of preparedness and the need to bring the light of truth into the world around him.[3]

It's been a precious time of encouragement to our sons, but it has also been a challenge to some of our family members as well. All of the generations before our children have been invited to speak or send a message, and it is a blessing how much thought and time everyone puts into it — including members of the extended family that don't share our convictions. All of them have had valuable things to say.

Food and fellowship end the celebration that day, but we follow it up with a serious attempt to keep our sons accountable for godly, manly behavior. We remind them they are supposed to be *men*, not children now. Obviously they don't have a man's responsibility nor his freedom yet, but they understand they have begun a transition to that status and we will be giving them as much as they show they can handle.

This is a marker for the beginning of new things. Over the next few years we work hard to identify and strengthen the remaining things in their growth and training prior to graduation. As they approach the end of high school, we look for the emergence of a mature, self-controlled young man, ready to face the world and stand for truth on his own. It will be time then for us to step back a bit and let him move to leadership in his own life.

Stepping Forward

When our eldest began to make college visits (we'll talk more about college and alternatives later), we were well aware of the stereotype many have of a Christian homeschooled boy — one who is afraid to be his own man. We knew it wasn't remotely true, especially not for this son who just returned from three months on his own in China, but we also knew he only had a short time to make an impression. We talked about and role-played what would happen when we visited the college, but when we got there, we stepped to the background and let our son take the lead. He went forward first, he introduced himself, then introduced us, and then he asked the vast majority of the questions. This worked wonderfully for presenting him in the best light. It also drove home to him that this was *his* life, *his* education. He was going to have to take charge of it for himself, not wait for Mom or Dad to push him along.

When we lived in Louisiana we made a field trip to a site called Vermilionville, a reconstruction of an Acadian ("Cajun") settlement in the bayou country near Lafayette. One feature of traditional Cajun homes was the separate sleeping arrangements for the children. The daughters' room could only be entered through the parents' bedroom, and their single tiny window usually had a rose bush or some other spiny shrub underneath. Elopement or other adventures were not easily undertaken from either side of the windowsill.

The boys, on the other hand, usually slept in the attic loft, which often had an outside stairway. This so-called *garçonnière*, a French term referring to "bachelors' quarters," gave young men the freedom to come and go without disturbing the rest of the family. Presumably that was the reason for the thorn bushes at the neighbors' house. Still, it showed the Cajuns considered that boys still young enough to live at home were able to take on some of the responsibilities and privileges of being men.

This time of transition for our sons is our time to make sure they are really taking up the reins for themselves. When a military pilot hands over the aircraft to his co-pilot, he keeps his grip on the controls until the co-pilot takes the stick and gives it a back-and-forth movement, signalling he has the plane in hand. We need to stay in command until our sons have their hands steady on the controls too, but then we can back away and let them fly while we continue to observe and offer advice. We may need to set limits in some areas, like when we are paying for things or to maintain order within the household, but it's time for our sons to be their own men. They'll be responsible for their own decisions, which means they'll need to make up their minds and then live with the results. As we move from a directive to an advisory position, our respect for their new level of adulthood may help them accept our counsel, not reject it.

Like arrows in the hand of a warrior, / So are *the children of one's youth.*[4] We don't aim to hold on to our arrows all the way to the target. They're not push-pins, they're meant to fly. Our job is to shape and prepare the arrows so when they are released, they fly straight and true on their own. The time is coming when they will leave our quiver and depart on their life's mission, and we have to prepare them—and ourselves—for that launch.

Preparing to Provide

A prime goal for each of our sons is to be able to support himself and a family as well. We had very good reasons that we chose to homeschool our children. We also had good reasons to accept a large family if the Lord provided one, which He did. We hope our sons will make the same choices, and to facilitate them, we encourage our sons never to depend on their future wives' income but to plan on shouldering the entire burden.

That means the time during and after high school is one of intense preparation for a career. How can we prepare our sons to support their families?

The first and most obvious thing is to teach them to be men of character. Diligence and dependability are crucial to their work ethic. Our guys expect to work to support the family's mission and do not expect to see immediate reward. They do household tasks, help in our ministry and pitch in with the family business. It's what we all do to keep the family going and we tell them that all the time.

It's critical to hold sons accountable for getting the job done right, on time. We aren't doing them any favors if we allow them to be lazy or turn in shoddy work. To allow them to waste time or procrastinate is setting them up for some painful lessons in adulthood. They need to learn to see a job through, not intentionally overlook the last few corners. "Close enough for government work" is no ethic for a Christian. We often remind our boys that no one pays for poor work or late work more than once, not if they have a choice.

Boys want purpose and direction. By pointing them to the future consequences of the habits - good and bad - they are learning now, we help them gain a desire to do right. One of our sons has struggled with laziness all his life. Watching his older brother entering the adult world has been a wake-up call, especially the realization that his brother's choice of colleges depended largely on the financial aid he could earn — and that was a result of the hard work he'd put in before he ever applied to college. Now the younger son is a new man, seeking out a job on his own, saving his money for college, and working diligently on his schoolwork. He has a vision.

Melanie grew up in an entrepreneurial family. Her people have been businessmen for many generations in many fields and she desperately wants to pass on that spirit to our sons. As a result, we make sure that we are constantly putting things into a business context. "Would a customer pay for work like that?" when a job is done half-way or "How would a client react to that kind of customer service?" when the chef of the day gripes because someone requests no mayonnaise on their sandwich. Teaching our sons to think like businessmen will help them enormously if they have their own businesses, but it will also make them much more profitable employees.

How do we know if our sons will be business owners or professionals or farmers or soldiers? We can't, really. We can and should give them the basic preparation that should make them successful wherever they are placed, though. They should learn respect for authority, diligence, initiative, determination, financial savvy. Really, it's the manly virtues we've been discussing all along that make a man succeed.

One thing we need to recognize in all humility is that God creates the children he sends us. He may give Dad a son to follow in his footsteps at the old alma mater and into the same line of business, but maybe not. There's a good chance that He'll have other plans, and we need to be able to accept that and learn from it if necessary. We both studied engineering and science, so when our eldest son expressed an interest in law and economics, we had to learn a new way to evaluate colleges. ("Liberal arts? What are those?")

But how can we help them figure out what God wants them to do in their lives?

We try to speak up when we notice particular strengths in the boys and we discuss with them different ways those strengths could be used. It's very easy to pigeonhole students into rigid academic and career tracks; "You're good in math," they told us, "so you should be in engineering." The possibility that God might create a musician with a talent for calculus, or an attorney who is good with statistics, never entered into the discussion. Our eldest son was very good in math *and hated every minute of it.* An engineering major might have pleased ol' Dad, but it would have been a poor fit for our son.

Hal found a book by Marcus Buckingham, *Now Discover Your Strengths,* that opened his eyes to a different way of seeing careers in relation to talents. Buckingham's view is that each of us has particular strengths that, with cultivation, can become centers of excellence. We have other skills that might be built up to a certain point, but we'll never be outstanding in them—just acceptably good. Why waste the opportunity to really excel where our gifts actually are, he asks, in order to pursue the illusion that everyone can be trained to do anything well? This insight gave Hal the confidence to set out in new directions he'd never explored, and he's found some surprising and rewarding opportunities that don't match the degree on the wall.[5]

When we see certain tendencies and interests in our sons, we try to give them a variety of experiences that help them to judge for themselves. One son has always been interested in science and loved medical things; last summer he earned the money to send himself to a week long anatomy and physiology camp at a state university.[6] He loved it as much as he thought he would—how many teenagers ever get to work on a human cadaver?—but he saw many students who discovered there that medicine was *not* the field for them. Our doctor said some of his classmates in medical school only come to that realization after investing thousands of dollars and hours in the program. What a time and money savings to figure that out in high school!

Another child with an interest in economics attended a camp teaching free market business practices; he found he loved it even more than he expected.[7] Other young men we know have interned or volunteered with veterinarians, architects, or politicians. Any kind of real-world experience can help our sons confirm an early interest or narrow down the range of choices they face.

And we pray. A lot.

The Next Step

Once a son has an idea where God may be leading him in his life, it's important to help him to find how to get there. That will mean research. We need to remember that God made our sons unique with their own special talents to use in the world, and they need our help determining the best way to prepare for their future careers.

We don't believe that college or apprenticeship or military service or business are good or bad, per se. It would be sad if there were no Christian doctors, soldiers, technicians, builders, or graphic designers. We've known men in each of these professions that served God in their daily work and would make excellent role models for our sons. We do need to understand the very different paths each of them had to take to reach that point of service, though, and counsel our sons accordingly.

Recently a mother approached Hal at an event where he'd been speaking.

"You're an independent engineer?" she said. "How wonderful! My son is very interested in engineering. We don't believe in college, so we're trying to find an apprenticeship for him. Do you ever take on apprentices?"

Hal had to gently explain to her that you can't take an apprenticeship route to what he does. To practice as a private consultant, you have to hold a state license. To qualify for the professional license, Hal had to have a degree from an accredited engineering school, then pass an initial exam, then have several years of experience under a supervising engineer, and finally pass another exam. State laws simply don't allow an alternate path.

On the other hand, the idea that everyone needs to go to college is a politician's daydream. Higher education often translates into higher salaries, true — but usually because the highly-paid professionals are in fields that require years of training and carry greater professional responsibility. The fact is that many fields are best learned at the side of an experienced craftsman, and the expectation of a four-year college degree seems to be nothing more than a gatekeeping-exercise to streamline the hiring process. It cuts down on the applicant pool, you see.

For many young men, college is not the answer. We're excited to see the diversity of career options being encouraged in the homeschool community. Males often learn so well by seeing and doing, we think the growth in apprenticeship programs and encouragement in entrepreneurship is going to bless a lot of young men.

A young man entering an apprenticeship needs to learn to submit as appropriate and to be a hard worker. He also needs to learn when to overlook things he disagrees with and when to speak up — or when to leave the relationship. He needs to able to respond to unethical behavior on the part of other employees or even his employer. On the other hand, the young man needs to know how to cull ideas for his own business one day — and what is ethical to copy and what's not.

Some of our sons will become businessmen. An entrepreneurial boy may have a business going by the time he's graduating. A cousin of ours started a web design business in high school and paid his way through Stanford University with it; he is now a leader in social media marketing research. Those who won't go to college still need preparation. A young man headed this way should be learning accounting and finance, studying good business practices and salesmanship. He will need to learn boldness, initiative and how to keep going through discouragement. Learning how to save, be frugal and avoid debt will help him tremendously, too. What a fantastic time to take the plunge into your own business — when you have so little to lose!

The military is another option taken by many of our sons' friends. As a former officer, Hal knows the military can be a good career choice for some, but a young man considering the military should speak with Christian men who are or were in the services first. Once the Army had a recruiting slogan — "It's not just a job — it's an adventure." That is true to a point, but maybe it would be better to consider military service as a culture, and a very specific one that touches every aspect of daily life. Even an assignment where civilians and soldiers work side by side every day, doing basically the same job, presents the military member with challenges to our normal American lifestyle expectations. Decisions about where to live, when to change jobs, who to associate with and how, and even whether you can expect leave to attend a family member's funeral, are all tied down under the phrase "the needs of the service." Military members give up much of their personal freedom in order to better protect to freedom of the rest of us. Some of our sons, frankly, won't adjust to that sacrifice very well.

That "freedom of association" can be problematic, too. The off-duty life of a military member varies widely between assignments, commanders, and comrades in arms. Hal was blessed with fairly conservative colleagues, but he had friends who suffered under constant harrassment from the profane and promiscuous lives of their forced work associations. Some young men may relish the missionary opportunities; others may find the climate spiritually draining and the carnal temptations aimed at them—especially as enlisted men—difficult to withstand.

There are many positive things that can be said for military service, and Hal is glad for the time he spent in that role. However, it is crucially important that young men get beyond the slogans and the presentations of quota-driven recruiters to seriously and soberly consider the decision and the commitment. If God makes the call clear to him, He will also provide the strength to serve in this challenging but necessary field.

When College May Be The Answer

Others of our boys will feel called to academic or professional fields, and there is really almost no way to do that except through a college degree. Some parents are rightfully concerned that sending their young men off to a distant, impersonal institution may undo what they've tried to instill in their sons' lives. Studies suggest that many children raised in the church turn their backs on religion when they leave home. That has to be considered.

At the same time, though, we need to weigh our concerns and our sons' spiritual maturity in a biblically objective way. Recently a friend related a conversation she'd had with a young man. He was living at home, no job, no career aspirations, and seemed to be floundering.

"Have you considered going to college?" she asked.

"No!" he shot back. "I'm not going to college. I might lose my faith!"

He was twenty-six years old.

It is good and right to be concerned about protecting our souls and those of our children. Still, isn't there a time when a man can be, should be, expected to stand in his faith? It would seem that by his mid-twenties, a young man should know what he believes and be willing to stake his life on it. The temptations and attacks he might experience in college can also assail him at work or simply in the community.

This is why we work to raise real men. There is a time to protect our sons and a time for them to start protecting others. There is a time to teach and disciple and control the influences our sons face, then there is a time for them to instruct others and to meet those influences and conquer them. The trick is discerning when a young man is able to stand and helping him to choose his battles wisely. We've got a lot of options in this area and they all have advantages and disadvantages.

Christian or secular college?

The debate over choosing an intentionally Christian college instead of a secular institution has been around as long as there was a distinction. We say "intentionally" Christian, because frankly many colleges which started out as Christian institutions have lost their religious distinctives and can be more hostile to the young believer than some of the secular colleges!

There are a number of outstanding Christian universities around the country, and while some programs like engineering and law are rare, they are available if you are willing to travel. Liberal arts programs are the most common, as many of these colleges were founded to support seminaries and teacher training programs. The institutions range from tiny Bible colleges with a ministerial focus to academic powerhouses like Grove City College and Hillsdale College that even the secular media respects.

The foremost advantage of an intentionally Christian school is the Christ-focused culture and curriculum. A young believer will be challenged to grow deeper in his faith, not to give it up. Students at a secular institution are going to be confronted, sometimes in their very dorm rooms, with the impact of lives carried on in opposition to God's word. Like the young soldier, a student at a secular college is going to find substance abuse, sexual license, and infidelity of many kinds winked at, ignored, and in some cases, given official sanction by the college administration.

That's not to say that Christian colleges are free from sin. The strictly-homeschooled daughter of our pastor at an earlier church came home from a denominational college pregnant, in spite of codes of conduct which were meant to encourage upright behavior. We carry our sinful natures into every situation, and we will find ways to gratify them if the temptation is strong enough — regardless of the school we attend. Some students chafe under strictures which are meant to guard them; some young men resent rules they don't find in Scripture. However, the cultural expectations at a real Christian college will be more supportive of a young believer's faith and conduct, hands down. That has to be a primary factor in choosing a college.

One downside to the Christian colleges is low levels of financial aid. Few of them enjoy large endowments that fund need- and merit-based scholarships at other private schools, nor do they receive subsidies from tax dollars in many cases. Secular universities on the average will be easier to pay for, and some private colleges have instituted no-loan grant policies that may prevent students from going into debt for tuition. Even so, the spiritual climate of a given school may be so toxic no scholarship could ever balance it out.

One thing to always keep in mind is that, whether attending a Christian or a secular college, all teachers are subject to the judgment of Scripture. Proverbs 9:10 says that *The fear of the* LORD *is the beginning of wisdom, / And the knowledge of the Holy One is understanding.* Isaiah 8:20 points *To the law and to the testimony!* as the standard of instruction; *If they do not speak according to this word,* it is *because* there is *no light in them.* The Berean church in Acts 17:10-11 was commended because they *searched the Scriptures daily to find out whether these things were so.* We need to admonish our sons to always compare the words of their teachers with the unchanging word of God, whether that teacher stands in a pulpit, lectern, or any other platform. Where teachers show a rejection or ignorance of God's truth, their words have to be carefully sifted for the errors that will follow — because errors will be there. Common grace may allow us to learn a great deal from an unbeliever's expertise and experience, yet sometimes it's still best to seek another teacher.

Approaching College with Discernment and Strategem

When the decision to pursue college studies has been made, there are several things that can be done to reduce cost and address concerns about academic or social issues on campus. One popular approach is to challenge courses for credit, with or without attending class. It is possible to add up significant undergraduate credits through Advanced Placement or International Baccalaureate programs, though their curricula will have a strongly secular viewpoint. This is more of an issue in some subjects than others, and we took the approach that sharing the material with our high schooler allowed us to discuss the subject from a Christian perspective and suggest how to demonstrate mastery of the material on the exam without accepting its plainly unbiblical presuppositions.

Some students, once enrolled, find professors who allow them to take the final exam for a class and award credit if the test score proves understanding — whether the student learned the material elsewhere or by studying the textbook on his own. This is a case-by-case situation but it does happen.

Many colleges accept credit on the basis of the College Level Exam Program (CLEP). Not every college grants credit in every situation, though, so be proactive and make sure before investing the effort. When they do, CLEP can allow a student to place out of an introductory course, same money on tuition, and possibly be a means of avoiding redundant or heavily politicized classwork (freshman courses sometimes do more indoctrination than upper level classes).

Many families in our area utilize community colleges and begin in high school with dual enrollment. This is a very cost effective choice and can help get a lot of credits out of the way before high school is over. When thinking about dual enrollment, parents need to consider that the community college system is geared for adult learners, and their 15-year-old son may be surrounded by 40-year-old men and women as classmates. They may face some of the same academic or social challenges found in a typical state college.

Distance learning is another alternative growing in popularity. It allows a young man to work while getting a degree, sometimes he can get it faster, and definitely he'll experience less influence from the campus environment. Both of us have used forms of distance learning for graduate courses and found good and bad points; while some courses offer scheduling flexibility, generally there is limited face-to-face interaction with professors and other students. A student needs to be highly self-disciplined to excel in this kind of program.

Socially, students must be prepared to stand truly alone. Especially at a secular college, or a Christian-in-name-only one, students may face loneliness and even ostracism because of their faith, or more obviously, just their holy example. Even Christian student groups may be led by immature Christians that worry more about appealing to the world than pleasing Christ. Although the social scene can be just as difficult in the work environment, you can go home from work to spend time with family and like-minded friends. That's not really true at college or in the military. It is a wise investment in our son's peace to pay the premium for a single dorm room or an off-campus apartment if he doesn't have a likeminded friend to plan to room with. He needs a haven.

When considering whether to attend a college on campus, we recommend making every effort to actually visit in person. Avoid the big recruiting events, where hundreds of prospective students are herded around like cattle. Instead, go on a weekday, preferably while classes are in session. Make appointments to talk with admissions officers and financial aid advisors; seek out the head of the department your son would most likely choose for a major. Suggest your son ask to sit in on a class in his major interest. Be a skeptical buyer; you're considering a major investment of time and money that will have an influence on the rest of your son's life.

Also make a point to meet with campus ministers. This applies to Christian colleges, too; while Hal graduated from a state university, Melanie attended both state and Christian colleges, and they've seen both sides. Whether the danger is worldliness and unbelief on a secular campus or legalism and complacency at a Christian school, it is important to connect up with a serious campus ministry that can provide teaching, support, and accountability. A frank discussion with campus ministers can uncover problems as well as strengths in the college culture. Take the time to research area churches, too; will your student find fellowship and encouragement close by, or will it require some driving to reach a suitable congregation?

From what we've seen and experienced, a believing young man involved in a local church, part of a vibrant Christian student group, well prepared to stand alone and defend his faith, will stand the best chance to stay strong no matter where he is. When it comes to spiritual life, stragglers get eaten.

Becoming Counselors

As we help our sons make the transition to independent adulthood, we need to be prepared to see them move back and forth in their reliance on us. The first year our oldest was away, there were weeks he called home several times a day - a minute here and there between classes, or an hour or more pouring out his concerns in the evening. Other weeks we didn't hear from him at all and would check his Facebook account to make sure he was still alive. Unfortunately, at this stage much of the communication comes when they are facing hard times and need to reconnect for some unconditional love or for advice on coping. That's okay, though, because we're glad to help - even late at night when we're really tired. It's good they are seeking counsel from *us* and not comparing inexperiences with the other freshmen down the hall. The tendency of young adults to want counseling in the wee hours is inconvenient, you bet, but parents need to be available when they are. It's worth it.

Conclusion

If we protect our relationship with our sons by helping them become independent and stand on their own two feet rather than being over-controlling, we can continue to have a valued impact in their lives as counselors they can absolutely trust. This is so important as they find a mate, join in the ministry of a church, get started in a career, begin their family and establish themselves in the world. We'll be there to bless their marriage, to give welcome and/or needed advice, and to pray with and for them. How much better the relation of fellow believers and family than the tense and hostile interaction many young adults have with parents who weren't intentional in their preparation for helping their sons become adults.

We have been very grateful for the relationship we have with our sons so far. This book has been very easy to write because we've lived it first. We are not perfect parents. We have gotten a lot of good advice over the years and we've learned from some mistakes, too. Along the way, we've learned that applying the Word of God and the principles found there to every area of life leads to great blessing—not great ease, nor lots of money, nor free time really, but lots of adventure and lots of joy. We've come to love being the parents of boys and to enjoy seeing God make men out of them. We're excited to see how He will use them as they take their places in the world. We hope that they will be mighty warriors for God.

Years ago, our whole family was able to travel to China together. Although the government still enforces a "one-child policy" for most of its people, the heart of the Chinese is not in it. Wherever we traveled we were treated like celebrities. People lined up to take their pictures with our blond-headed children.

"Are you one family? Are they all your children?" they'd ask. We'd answer in our best limited Mandarin:

"Wǒ men yǒu qī ge xiǎo háir—liù ge ér zi-yi ge nǚér."

"We have seven children" we'd say, "- six sons—one daughter." They invariably responded, "Lucky family! Happy family! Fortunate family!" and very often someone would say, "Hero mother!"

In our society, we think it takes a hero to raise a son because they are so difficult - aggressive, reckless, noisy, independent, just hard to manage. We don't think that is what our Chinese observers meant. We think they meant that the mother of a son has a wonderful opportunity — that she may become a *mother of heroes*.

May we all become the parents of godly heroes.

Notes for Chapter 14

[1] Exodus 20:12. The command appears eight times in Scripture.

[2] Ephesians 6:1

[3] True to form, when Hal was suddenly called to Saudi Arabia on an emergency engineering project, Matthew's flashlight was the best one available in the house. It went to the Middle East and put light into some very dark corners indeed.

[4] Psalm 127:4

[5] Marcus Buckingham and Donald Clifton, *Now Discover Your Strengths* (New York: The Free Press, 2001). This is best read after reading his earlier book, *First Break All The Rules* (co-authored by Curt Coffman). The first book deals with excellent managers, while *Strengths* focuses more on excellent individuals.

[6] This was Greg Landry's Anatomy & Physiology Camp held at Appalachian State University in Boone, N.C. See his website at www.anatomycamp.com for more information.

[7] The Free Enterprise Leadership Challenge is a project of the Jesse Helms Center in Wingate, N.C. FELC has taken the program to other college campuses, to high schools in Latin America, and in various formats to conferences and other events. For more information about this outstanding program, see the Helms Center website at http://www.jessehelmscenter.org

Appendix

But My Son Isn't....

A fter our workshops on raising boys, the first question is almost always the same: "None of this applies to my son," someone says. "He doesn't like dirt. He's very fearful and sensitive. He's dramatic and artsy. How can I meet his needs?"

God did not make everyone the same. Some are made to be loggers, some doctors, some accountants. Differences in preferences are normal. Some boys are more sensitive, others are thick-skinned. Some are more fearful, others are bold by nature. Some love dirt, but others are fastidious. How about the boys that don't seem to fit into the most common traits we've described?

A Man's a Man

W e've got to remember that a little boy like that still has far more in common with his father or brother or uncle than he does his mother and sisters. Every single cell in his body (well, except for the germ line cells that will enable him to father a child) has one X-chromosome and one Y. He is 100% male. His maleness may not show itself just the same way or he might be more hesitant to express it, but God made him a boy and he should be raised with that in mind. He should be encouraged to be happy God made him the way he is.

One of the things we've done to encourage our sons who have done some unusual things is to always describe what they are doing in manly terms. Our son who loves to bake bread and cook omelets would be tonight's "chef," for example. Our son who loves to draw is given examples like Rembrandt and DaVinci. A son who repairs his own jeans is a great "tailor," never a seamstress. For goodness' sake, they're called "Levis" because they were invented by a man named Levi Strauss — for miner's clothing. Good, tough, manly stuff. Make sure that you see your son as a man in training, and help him see himself that way.

We also keep an eye out for manly virtues to praise in our sons, and particularly those who are not coming off in a very manly way right now. For example, a little boy who goes downstairs in the dark to fetch something is praised for his courage, not sympathized with for his fearfulness. A young brother who is whacked by his sister is praised for his manly restraint in not hitting a girl. A boy who does a job for his mother before she asks is praised for showing initiative. By praising the manly virtues, we encourage our sons in the development of that kind of character.

Challenging Him

Sometimes our sons need to be stretched. Recently, one of our younger sons was feeling a little left out by his older brothers. They are all about football right now and they are so much bigger than he is, it's intimidating to think about jumping into the fray. We encouraged his brothers to find a way to include him - to teach him how to pass and catch and find a way he could join in.

Initially, he was afraid the ball would hurt him, but his brother encouraged him to throw it as hard as he could at his brother.

"See, that didn't hurt a bit. Let me throw it at you. I'll start really easy."

Once the ball hit him and it didn't hurt, he grew in confidence. They started out with him right in front of them and tossed the ball gently right into his hands. If he caught it, he took a step forward; if not, he took a step back. They promised him a treat if he got to a point about 20 feet away. Once he was catching all right, they brought him into a game. They made him the quarterback and told him exactly what to do. I was amazed to see him get tackled or knocked down and jump right up again. He had faced his fear, found it wasn't as bad as he thought, and was set free to play.

We look for areas where our sons are fearful, encourage them to confront those fears and praise them profusely when they do, even when they aren't entirely successful. Like everything else, we do this step by step with incentives for persistence. A son who's afraid to go into the dark part of the house late at night would still be given the errand, but we might send an older brother with him, "to help you reach the shelf," *not* mentioning it's to give him company. A son who's squeamish might be asked to kill a bug for his mother, "Please be a man and help me - I just hate bugs." When he does, he'll find it's not so bad, and he'll really enjoy protecting his mother.

One of our boys was afraid of the water and didn't want to learn to swim, but really wanted to learn how to use the kayak.

"I'm sorry son, but you can't swim. That just wouldn't be safe. Would you like to learn to swim?"

On reflection, he rather thought he would. And he handles the kayak really well now.

Giving Permission

Sometimes our sons need permission to get dirty or get tough or be manly. Often a son so wants to please his mother that he'll avoid dirt or rough play to avoid upsetting her to the point he's not comfortable with it either.

Sometimes a son just misunderstands our admonitions. One of our sons came home from a community event just crushed. He'd been bullied and tormented all day by a boy who was amusing himself by frightening the younger children. The bully threatened to punch our son out when he went to the bathroom, so he didn't want to go back the next day. He asked his father if he had to go back.

"Dad, what do I do?"

Hal told him that if the boy punched him to let him have it.

"But Dad, you tell us all the time not to fight."

"Young man, you have no need to fight with your brothers. They are not going to hurt you and your parents are always there to step in. Son, we don't ever want you to start a fight, but if someone else starts one, *you end it*."

"But Dad, he's two years older and a head taller than me."

That's exactly why we told him to fight back. A bigger child or an adult who tries to hurt a younger child should be resisted. Like an adult, a child should turn the other cheek to his peers and siblings, but a bully trying to hurt a weaker person needs to be stopped.

He needed encouragement at this point.

"Son, I'm sure he doesn't have five brothers he wrestles with all the time. I'll bet you are tougher than he is. Bullies are usually cowards."

The next day, as soon as Melanie saw him, she knew something had happened. He was calm, confident and happy.

"Mom! When I went to the bathroom, he followed me. He and his friend cornered me and he punched me in the stomach. It wasn't as bad as I thought it would be! I just hauled off and punched him back in the stomach, then on the chin," he said. "You wouldn't believe it! He just fell down on the floor and started crying. I'd barely hit him, but he was saying, 'I didn't know you were so tough! Please don't hurt me!' What a baby! He never picked on anybody else all day. Everybody kept wondering what had happened to stop him. I just smiled."

Our son just needed permission to defend himself. He thought he was being a good boy by tolerating that abuse and living with that fear.

Our boys need to be comfortable in their own skins. Not all men are athletes just like not all are intellectuals. Manliness is much more than brute force, it's a heart attitude of confidence and boldness to accomplish the mission given by God. All of our sons can have that; we can be the ones to give it to them.

Acknowledgements

"No man is an island unto himself," said John Donne. Anyone involved in writing a book will find more and more people drawn into the spiraling vortex of the project. We are duty bound to recognize the contributions of these longsuffering people, many of whom had no idea what they were getting into.

First, thanks to our friends Joseph and Teresa Wirtz, whose counsel on an upcoming convention led to our first steps getting the book out of our heads and on paper.

A big hoo-ah to fellow author Mary S. Roper, who suggested the title we adopted when the book grew past its original scope.

Longtime friend and tireless support group leader Cathy Jones was our proofreader. She gave us frank, concise, and rapid responses to the book we emailed her chapter by chapter. One would think that a document written and reviewed through four and five revisions by two published writers would be logical, readable, and error free at that point. One would be wrong, it seems. Thanks, Cathy. Hal says you can keep the extra commas you found but please return the semi-colons when you can.

We also would like to recognize our friends Curt and Sandra Lovelace and Tami Fox, all of them experienced editors, whose numerous detailed suggestions improved the text at many points.

To our eldest son John Calvin Young, the son whose name appears most often in the text, thanks for your good spirit about sharing your adventures growing up at the head of this pack. We owe you even more thanks for your help typesetting the book, through airports, freeways, living rooms and upper bunks. It looks just like we want.

To Caleb, a still-new driver who braved rush-hour traffic behind the wheel in Philadelphia and New York, so John could complete typesetting, and Matthew, who gave up his laptop and his own writing project so Melanie could work on the book, while holding a high-need baby.

To our other sons and daughters, who held the baby, cooked, cleaned, or stayed out of the way while the book was being finished — thanks for understanding. Mom and Dad will be with you in a moment.

To Erica Palmisano, our graphic designer — thanks for providing us with a terrific cover design on basically zero notice, literally in the final days before we went to press. You took a critical missing part of the project and made it, as our Chinese family members would say, *Bú máfan* — not a problem. Whew.

To our extended family and many friends whose anonymous anecdotes helped illustrate our point here and there — you know who you are and we won't tell. Thanks for being part of our lives.

And finally, thanks to the thousands of homeschoolers who have heard us speak on several of these topics, particularly Melanie's original presentation, "Ballistic Homeschooling." The encouragement and feedback you gave us led directly to the present volume. We hope God has blessed whatever advice we may have shared and we look forward to hearing from you again.

INDEX

Colophon

This book is set in 12-point Gentium Book Basic Regular with 14.4-point leading, a "typeface for the nations" designed by Victor Gaultney. The display face is 14 and 18-point Orlando.

The main text was laid out in Adobe InDesign CS4 with optical margins and glyph extension algorithms applied. The cover was designed by Erica Palmisano.